Basic Cost Benefit Analysis for Assessing Local Public Projects

Basic Cost Benefit Analysis for Assessing Local Public Projects

Second Edition

Barry P. Keating and Maryann O. Keating

Basic Cost Benefit Analysis for Assessing Local Public Projects,
Second Edition

Copyright © Business Expert Press, LLC, 2017.

First published in 2014 by
Business Expert Press, LLC
222 East 46th Street, New York, NY 10017
www.businessexpertpress.com

ISBN-13: 978-1-63157-881-6 (paperback)
ISBN-13: 978-1-63157-882-3 (e-book)

Business Expert Press Economics Collection

Collection ISSN: 2163-761X (print)
Collection ISSN: 2163-7628 (electronic)

Cover and interior design by Exeter Premedia Services Private Ltd., Chennai, India

Second edition: 2017

10 9 8 7 6 5 4 3 2 1

Printed in the United States of America.

Abstract

Cost benefit analysis (CBA) is often expected or required for government projects. On the state and local level, the technique is useful for assessing the worthiness of a specific policy proposal. The accounting and analysis of large-scale technical projects require specialized training; in this manual, we offer a nontheoretical introduction to CBA, accessible to readers without an advanced statistical or economic background. The book is designed as a how-to primer in the basics of CBA for local officials who actually evaluate proposals or merely interpret reports using CBA. A Reference List is provided for further study.

There is a critical need for officials and the general public to question assumptions, biases, and omissions in proposals submitted by those advocating for certain projects. Tax revenue is limited and government debt at some point becomes unsustainable. CBA is rooted in and has little or no value apart from the economic concepts of cost and resource efficiency, but our goal here is not to stress underlying economic theory. Rather, this manual is designed to explain the correct use and interpretation of CBA, pointing out CBA's limitations and pitfalls.

Properly employed, CBA is simply a method for assessing a proposal prior to a collective-choice decision. The CBA process uncovers and measures the intensity of values that residents place on certain services. It attempts to measure net benefits to be derived from a specific proposal relative to an alternative project or the default option of doing nothing. Because standard statistical packages, spreadsheets, and graphical analyses are now generally available, CBA, as a tool, has become more accessible for small projects on a local level. Case studies, presented in the final chapters of this book, represent typical proposals confronted by local officials. Included are instructions for using computer spreadsheets to build basic cost benefit models and an Appendix on the step-by-step process for discounting future costs and benefits.

Completing this book will allow a student or local government decision maker to understand and construct a simple CBA model. They will also be able to evaluate more extensive CBA models for accuracy and shortcomings.

Keywords

benefits ratio, cost benefit analysis (CBA), cost effectiveness analysis, discount rate, economic efficiency, existence values, external or social benefits, external or social costs, externalities or spillovers, government failure, hedonic valuation, hypothetical contingent valuation, local government, market failure, net discounted benefits, positive time preference, present value of benefits, present value of costs, project evaluation, regulatory capture, rent seeking, sensitivity analysis, social welfare functions, standing, willingness to accept, willingness to pay

Contents

CHAPTER 1

An Introduction to Cost-Benefit Analysis

The very need to weigh benefits against costs-the essence of economics-is evaded by the irresponsible exercise of arrogance.

—Thomas Sowell

Chapter 1 Preview

When you have completed reading this chapter you will:

- see this book as a practical guide for decision-makers charged either with performing or interpreting basic cost-benefit analysis (CBA);
- be aware of project proposals for which CBA is and is not an appropriate decision tool;
- know why government project assessment requires different tools than private project assessment;
- realize that objective decision making is based on considering foregone options, minimizing costs, and using scarce resources to produce what residents need and desire;
- be able to explain why CBA is a useful tool for determining net benefits based on the difference between discounted benefits and discounted costs;
- refer to available statistics for your particular local government unit;
- know how to discount future costs and benefits using a spreadsheet;
- realize that collective decision-making, with respect to a specific government proposal, ultimately depends on the choice of the voting public.

Introduction

It is a truth universally acknowledged that any project proposed to local government is in want of a good justification. In too many instances, only well-meaning intentions suffice. It is odd that public projects, in contrast to private corporate investments, are often devoid of simple decision-making rules. There is a way, however, for local officials and residents to rank and evaluate modest public proposals without commissioning costly feasibility studies. In modified form, CBA methodology has a role in ruling out egregious, unrealistic proposals.

Suppose that you were one of nine Common Council Members of a mid-sized town. The main business at the next Council meeting is to read for the second time a Bill forwarded to the Council for consideration and approval by the mayor and the Community and Economic Development Committee. The Bill represents a plan to be implemented by the city, the nonprofit Northside Neighborhood Association, and a private for-profit corporation working together to develop the housing stock in a strategic area of the city. The goal is to improve the quality of present owner-occupied properties, to renovate viable homes for resale and as rentals, and to demolish vacant and abandoned structures.

The proposal requests that $9 million be allocated to the program in equal installments over the next 5 years. The source of funds would be city tax revenue, the state foreclosure prevention program, and federal government's block grants for community development and neighborhood stabilization. A total of 100 properties would be affected by the program. The city would retain ownership of 50 vacant and abandoned properties until sold on behalf of the city prior to the program completion in 10 years. Another 50 dwellings would be rehabilitated. Increased property values are expected to generate additional property taxes to finance infrastructure and policing throughout the city.

As a hypothetical council member you are undecided on voting to approve the mayor and development committee's proposed bill. Distressed by the number of decaying properties in town, you, nevertheless, act in trust for a district outside the targeted area. A quick calculation ($9 million divided by 100 properties) suggests that per property cost of $90,000 exceeds the average price of homes throughout the city. You are not an expert in law, finance, or construction, and there are so many variables to consider. What technique would allow you to get a handle on voting rationally in the present and long-term best interests of the city? CBA is an option, worthy of serious consideration.

CBA is an exercise leading decision-makers to list and quantify in monetary terms all costs and benefits associated with a proposal. Assessing costs and benefits is resisted, understandably. It is emotionally difficult to accept that certain benefits, particularly the value of human life, be evaluated and quantified. In addition, we are legitimately cautious about any analysis that can be easily skewed in favor of personal interests. Yet, accountability requires public officials, as well as agency administrators, to deal with the question, "What value do residents receive in return for projects subsidized with taxpayer funds?"

Corporations, in maximizing profits, rely on benefits per dollar to differentiate between projects. Unfortunately, such tools do not translate well into the government sector. In the case of public goods and services, those who benefit do not necessarily purchase them, and those who finance them do not necessarily consume them. Also, in both the non-profit and government sectors, users generally do not pay fees covering the full cost of providing the goods and services offered.

CBA is an appropriate tool for estimating a project's net direct and indirect benefits received regardless of who pays the bill or who receives the benefits. In assessing public project proposals, CBA attempts explicitly to account for external (public) effects in addition to personal (private) costs and benefits. External effects refer to those costs and benefits affecting all members, not just those who are the primary providers or recipients. For example, students and their parents, the primary beneficiaries of publicly funded K-12 education, are charged nominal fees with the remaining amount financed by community funded endowments plus federal, state, and local tax revenues.

In this book, we reserve the term CBA to government-financed projects, but elsewhere this method is referred to as "social cost benefit analysis." We prefer the simple term "cost benefit analysis (CBA)" and use it both in reference to infrastructure-type projects such as highways as well as those dealing with social concerns such as housing, education, and health.

Federal agencies struggle with mandates requiring them to provide cost-benefit analysis for all proposals above a certain cost. If large federal bureaucracies struggle with it, how can we argue here for CBA's applicability in assessing modest local government projects? If CBA is such an appropriate tool, why is it so seldom applied? The answer to both questions is that CBA is based on economic theory that is sometimes difficult to understand and even more difficult to operationalize; undoubtedly it is easier to make decisions based on emotions and political expediency. In essence, we repeat, CBA is simply a standardized method to fully account for all costs associated with a new proposal along with a detailed calculation of specific private and public benefits. Properly employed, CBA determines whether or not a proposal should be considered and attempts to calculate net benefits relative to an alternative project or the default option of doing nothing.

Government guidelines are essential for CBA but, at this point, are still in the developmental stage. However, CBA templates may be found in governmental handbooks and in reports that have been contracted out to corporate consultants. At present, these handbooks and reports (listed in the "Suggestions for Further Reading" section in this book) are good reference sources, but fail in providing a level of transferable standards accessible to those engaged in local government decision making.

We call attention to the gap between high church CBA, so to speak, and the need, on the other hand, for rudimentary CBA required by local officials to self-assess local projects. CBA is often out-sourced to professional consultants, raising costs and eliminating its use for all but mega-projects. We maintain that there is a role for making CBA accessible and understandable to those, appraising small-scale public projects, who possess undergraduate levels of numerical and economic proficiency. Furthermore, case studies, for similar projects in comparable communities, are helpful and these can often be replicated or modified to gain CBA expertise.

As CBA techniques and additional data become available, the cost of performing CBA should fall. Statistical packages, spreadsheets, and databases are more accessible to local officials and ordinary residents than at any previous time. The CBA method should be presented as one tool among others to effectively combine computational tools and available data to assess any proposed intervention involving tax revenue.

When CBA Is an Appropriate Tool

CBA provides helpful advice for decisions involving infrastructure in government buildings, roads, public housing, sewage, and water treatment as well as for programs dealing with public safety, education, health, leisure, welfare reform, employment, and child protection. CBA is also used in assessing regulatory impact. In other words, CBA is useful in considering the potential impact of any project that changes the prevailing use of a community's scarce resources currently available to both the public and private sectors. The benefits and costs of any project impact all members of the community for whom the decision makers act in trust.

It is essential not to assign to CBA functions exceeding its capability. CBA, particularly on a local level, is an inappropriate tool for analyzing income distributional goals, the incidence of various taxes, or in addressing questions associated with property or personal rights. It does not, for example, help in assigning the degree of entitlements to certain levels of health care or education.[1]

The CBA Decision Rule

At all levels of complexity, CBA reduces to the simple diagram presented in Figure 1.1. Figure 1.1 shows that the minimal acceptance criterion for any proposal is that the value of net benefits be greater than zero. Net benefits are equal to the present value of benefits minus the present value of costs.

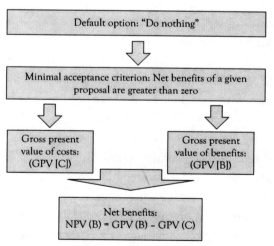

Figure 1.1 An overview of CBA minimal acceptance criterion for any proposed intervention is that the present value of net benefits, equal to the present value of benefits minus the present value of costs, be greater than zero.

The framework for CBA is a straightforward calculation of net benefits expected from implementing a proposal. Each proposal has a specific time horizon and addresses the costs and benefits defined in terms of the constituency for which the decision maker has fiduciary responsibility. The base line in considering whether or not to accept a proposal is the default option of doing nothing. The concept of present value is presented in a tutorial in the Appendix. In subsequent chapters, we proceed with the task of quantifying public and private costs and benefits. We begin here by examining the roots of CBA within economic theory.

CBA and Economic Efficiency

Because this book deals with the assessment of relatively small local projects, we can legitimately ignore the complexities of economic growth models and macroeconomic stabilization. On the other hand, an intuitive microeconomic understanding of opportunity costs and of economic efficiency is essential for CBA. Ironically, there is no analytical distinction between benefits and costs. A benefit is a net gain that accrues either in a monetary form or in well-being to any individual included in the relevant group. Opportunity costs are simply benefits foregone in some other activity by using resources required for the proposed project in some alternate way.[2] Consider the hypothetical city project, previously discussed, to rehabilitate, over 10 years, 100 properties at a cost of $9 million. This cost represents x number of miles of that will not be resurfaced or $9 million in private consumption forfeited by households. CBA compares this $9 million cost, representing lost opportunities, with the monetary value of expected benefits resulting from the rehabilitated properties.

Rational local decision making starts with assuming that there are mutual values or goals held in common by residents and a means to reconcile conflicts through voting and democratic processes.[3] We take this legal framework for local government as given. CBA, then, is a means for ensuring that an area's limited resources are not wasted or squandered.

In order to understand the economic assumptions of CBA, place yourself in the shoes of a member of the South Bend Board of Public Works.

A plan to shelter up to 60 homeless men from December 1 to April 1 was submitted to South Bend Common Council, and, on the following morning, the Board of Public Works was expected to consider the proposal (Blasko, Erin. "City to Buy Building for Homeless," The South Bend Tribune, Tuesday, October 25, 2016, A1).

According to the plan, presented by the Department of Community Investment, the city would pay up to $125,000 to purchase a building across the alley from Hope Ministries' Project WARM, a weather amnesty program providing overnight shelter to homeless individuals living on the street during the winter.

Project WARM is willing to contribute $45,000 for staffing and general maintenance, and Hope Ministries as much as $30,000 for long-term maintenance and rehab. Hope Ministries, the South Bend Center for the Homeless, and Life Treatment facilities, are all private nonprofits with experience in providing these services locally, but anticipate limited excess capacity for men, women, and families. Last winter over 50 people were living on the street, but the number is expected to increase (not to exceed 100) this year.

Could CBA assist you as a Public Works Board member having to make a quick decision on spending $125,000 in tax dollars for this proposal? No doubt, you are well aware that private households could benefit from retaining these funds for personal needs and also that the revenue may be better allocated to other public projects. And do not forget that the contributing nonprofits will need to cut back on alternate projects. A $125,000 tax expenditure forfeits economic value that perhaps could be better used elsewhere. If the Board approves this proposal, can you be certain something of equal or greater value than opportunities lost will be created?

The issue, then, is regardless of which residents are receiving the benefits or paying costs, does the proposal being considered meet your back-of-the-envelope calculation of positive net benefits.

The total cost of the proposal is estimated at $200,000 ($125,000 paid in tax revenue for a property with no residual value to the city and $75,000 in private nonprofit contributions). The facility would be open by December 1 and close its doors in approximately 120 days. If the facility, designed for 60, averaged 50 men per night, the shelter would offer lodging for 6,000 nights. This works out to about $34 a night per occupant ($200,000/6,000).

Overestimation of needed beds could easily double costs per person in which case distributing hotel vouchers could be a better approach. If, however, the estimate of 50 residents per night is in the ball park, you, as a voting Board member, need to determine if the per person per night value is approximately $34. In subsequent chapters, methods of determining the dollar value of benefits will be explored. Homeless residents, valuing their health on severely cold nights, may voluntarily seek shelter in the facility; this choice indicates that the shelter would create some private value. However, in addition, you need to determine the public good value in terms of the ethical, safety, and health benefits for town residents in general if the homeless could be legally directed to shelter this winter. If the sum of private benefits to the homeless and public benefits equals or exceeds $34 per person per night, this shelter proposal would pass the positive net benefits hurdle. Economic efficiency lies at the crux of CBA, as indicated by the following three assumptions.

First, every accepted proposal has an opportunity cost, measured in units of local currency adjusted for inflation. Funds expended represent the value of a community's scarce resources; all funds used to provide the shelter, in the example given, could be used for other purposes. Limited and valued inputs will be reallocated if the project is approved.

Second, any good or service provided locally must consider cost effectiveness. Consider a worthy goal, such as the preservation of historic buildings. CBA along with a related methodology, cost effectiveness, can uncover excessively high marginal costs for restoring and preserving, for example, certain decrepit structures deemed to have historical value. Such proposals can be rejected and alternatives considered on the grounds of cost effectiveness with respect to the overall benefits to residents of preserving a community's history. This does not preclude private individuals, with a great appreciation for antiquities, expending enormous private resources on preservation.

Finally, CBA takes as a given that at this time and place there is an optimal limit to the production of any good, public or private, based on the public's willingness to pay. A particular community, for example, may express a willingness to publicly subsidize 1 or 2 historical structures in center city, but not 8 or 10. Preferences can be assessed, for example, by noting current attendance at such sites or a willingness to pay entrance fees.

Aside from its own operational expenses, government spending may be classified as either allocative or distributive. Allocative activities involve shifting resources between the private and public sectors of the economy or within the public sector. Distributive activities, presently the largest component of the Federal budget, involve social programs that transfer income between households in order to reduce the variance of income. Recall that our primary focus is on overall resource allocations including activities such as education, training, and recreation which can have income-distributing effects. However, the goal of CBA is not necessarily to equalize household incomes.

Impossibility of Pleasing All Residents All the Time

The lack of unanimity in government decision making and the coercive aspect of taxation are serious issues. CBA makes no pretense of being able to solve these difficulties.

Some readers may be familiar with a decision rule to approve any program, believed to improve the well-being of society, if it makes at least one person better off and no one worse off. Obviously, this rules out most local projects using tax revenue, which is involuntary and results in harm (higher taxes) to some individuals. In CBA, those who pay the cost are not necessarily those who receive the benefits; therefore, this decision rule leaves CBA, so to speak, up the creek without a paddle. Fortunately, an alternative view, compatible with CBA, requires only that project beneficiaries be able to compensate losers and still remain better off. Note that the modification says that gainers should be able to compensate losers, not that they must. This conflict will be discussed again in Chapter 2 in reference to social welfare theory; economists use the term social welfare to mean the overall well-being of society.

Deciding Between Projects

Decision makers are often forced to choose between worthwhile projects. The obvious solution is to select the alternative that produces the greatest net benefit. For simplification, we do not extend our analysis to multiple options; our analysis stops with determining if a particular project being considered yields positive net benefits.

Rudimentary CBA relies on an analyst's acceptance of revealed preferences. How people actually behave in markets, surveys, and voting indicates how resources should be directed to maintain or improve the well-being of the local community. Mistakes are inevitable. Furthermore, it is recognized that the amount of a public good provided and the cost per person does not reflect the preference of all, or even one person. At most, these decisions ultimately represent more or less the preferences of a median voter. This does not preclude elected representatives acting on behalf of a constituency. CBA is merely a tool for officials, acting in trust for others, to determine if a particular project yields benefits for which residents are willing to pay, at costs they are willing to accept.

CBA is never a substitute for thought and judgment. But, by making decisions explicit and, to some degree, quantifiable, CBA clarifies and introduces a degree of rigor and rationality into local government policy. Any rejection of CBA methodology is a rejection of rationality in public policy. Indeed, it may be the relatively simple and straightforwardness of CBA that preclude its adoption. Projects offering a small benefit to many are abandoned, whereas a subgroup anticipating a large gain comes to the table prepared to advocate and gain approval for their favored proposals.

Public Goods Versus Private Goods

Individuals choose to purchase or not to purchase private goods available in markets. On the other hand, projects considered by government decision makers share, to some degree, at least one of two public good characteristics, **nonexclusivity** and **nonrivalry**. **Nonexclusivity** means that it would be prohibitively expensive or impossible to exclude anyone from consuming a good or service once provided. Police protection is one example having this characteristic. **Nonrivalry** means that one person's consumption does not limit the consumption of others. For example, your enjoyment of a center-city fountain does not reduce someone else's enjoyment of the same fountain. Lighthouses are one of the best examples of a pure public good, because they are characterized by both nonexclusivity and nonrivalry.

Generally, projects, having one or both public good characteristics, are not and would not be optimally provided in private (nongovernment) markets. That is why decisions about public goods and services are made in city hall rather than in the shopping mall. We interpret CBA as a descriptive and informational tool providing information to a government decision maker allocating tax or donor revenue to specific projects. CBA informs, but does not choose; the final go-ahead on any project is determined by direct referendum or by officials operating in trust for the local community. CBA, calculating the present value of benefits minus costs, points decision makers toward those activities and projects yielding positive net benefits.

CBA in the Context of Local Constraints

It is conceivable that officials select projects from a comprehensive list ranking net benefits and, in this way, maximize total net benefits. However, this text is oriented to a yea or nay decision regarding a specific proposal. Before implementing CBA, it is worthwhile to perform an assessment of local conditions. Because the decision will be made in the context of a specific local environment, a particular project could meet CBA's positive net benefit criterion and still not be a good fit for a particular community.

Within the 50 states in the United States, the U.S. Census Bureau in 2007 counted 39,044 general purpose local governments: 19,492 municipal, 16,519 township, and 3,033 county governments. In addition, there are 50,087 special purpose independent decision making units, such as schools or economic-development districts, each allocating tax revenue. You can find actual data for your own state, county, or town at quick-facts.cenus.gov. On this website, statistics for every state, county, and city in the United States can be found. Table 1.1 is a sample of available data showing both the uniqueness and comparability of each locality.

Table 1.1 A Sample of available data demonstrating both the uniqueness and comparability for each locality

	State of Washington	Ferry County, WA	Battle Ground (Clark Co), WA	State of Indiana	Clark County, IN	Bloomington (Monroe Co). IN	State of Florida	Clay County, FL	Aventura (Miami-Dade Co). FL
Population, 2015 estimate	7,170,351	7,582	19,407	6,619.680	115,371	84,067	20,271.272	203,967	37,649
High school graduate or higher, percent of persons age 25+, 2011–2015	90.40%	87.30%	89.90%	87.80%	87.20%	93%	86.90%	90%	93.80%
Bachelor's degree or higher, percent of persons age 25+, 2011–2015	32.90%	16.70%	20.70%	24.10%	20.10%	57.20%	27.30%	23.80%	52.00%
Homeownership rate, 2011–2015	62.50%	71.20%	66.80%	69.00%	71.10%	33.70%	65.30%	74.80%	67.00%
Median value of owner-occupied housing units, 2011–2015	$ 259,500	$ 166,000	$ 210,800	$ 124,200	$ 129,000	$ 173,400	$ 159,000	$ 153,000	$ 300,600
Households, 2011–2015	2,668,912	3,103	5,989	2,501,937	42,974	30,232	7,300.494	69,053	18,701
Persons per household, 2011–2015	2.56	2.39	3.09	2.55	2.59	2.27	2.63	2.84	1.99
Percent of persons in civilian labor force, 16+ years, 2011–2016	63.5	43.2	64.5	63.9	65.5	56.7	58.8	62.3	54.8
Per capita money income in the past 12 months (2014 dollars), 2011–2015	$ 31,762	$ 20,602	$ 22.301	$ 25,346	$ 25,470	$ 19,786	$ 26,829	$ 26,464	$ 49,290
Median household income, 2011–2015	$ 61,062	$ 38,125	$ 58.525	$ 49.255	$ 51,699	$ 30,019	$ 47,507	$ 58,290	$ 60,222
Persons in poverty, percent estimate	12%	20.4%	13.4%	14.5%	10.4%	38%	15.7%	11.6%	11.6%

Source: US Census Bureau State and County Quick Facts

Each state, county, and town is necessarily constrained by its present circumstances. With back-of-the-envelope calculations, it is possible to identify and project the economic framework for a given population, its potential tax revenue, and the level of sustainable public debt that can be reasonably serviced. We do not recommend that local CBA attempt to achieve economic stabilization or direct growth. Local administrators, at best, can accept, maintain, or perhaps nudge a community onto its potential annual growth path, which in most times and places operates somewhere in a range between -5 to +5 percent. Local policies are effective, however, in creating or destroying an environment conducive to growth. CBA assists local officials with their responsibility of keeping constituencies informed of tradeoffs between various alternatives.

Skills Required for CBA

CBA typically involves mathematical calculations done in spreadsheets. A good place to begin learning the CBA technique is with the present value tutorial presented in the Appendix.

Any two net benefit calculations, performed by separate analysts, are unlikely to be identical, as CBA is both art and science. Nevertheless, separate studies generally consistently confirm net benefits to be either positive or negative. Sensitivity analysis, to be fully explained in Chapter 3, is an additional means of dealing with uncertainty, especially when net benefits are relatively small. Sensitivity analysis is a method whereby an analyst solves for expected net benefits with different assumptions about discount rates, number of clients, and so forth. Even when sensitivity yields inconsistent conclusions, such information is valuable and often results in better more realistic reports. In this manner, CBA permits an analyst to confidently explain how he or she determined that a given proposal be considered or summarily rejected.

The hallmark of CBA is to accurately appraise a project in monetary terms as the difference between a community's propensity to pay for a public good minus its opportunity cost. As a method, however, it should be valued not strictly in terms of its precision but rather in making project appraisals more realistic than otherwise presented.

Summary of What You Have Learned in Chapter 1

- You can define Cost Benefit Analysis (CBA) as a tool for providing information to officials entrusted with evaluating projects funded with tax revenue or government debt.
- You can refer to and interpret a formula for calculating the net present value of benefits (NPV [B]) as the difference between gross present value of benefits (GPV [B]) and the gross present value of cost (GPV [C]).
- You can discount future costs and benefits based on the example presented in the Appendix to this text using the Excel spreadsheet NPV formula.
- You can recognize the minimum criterion for considering a proposal (i.e., a net benefit).
- You can evaluate CBA in terms of its goal of economic efficiency defined in terms of cost effectiveness and scarce factor allocation.
- You can explain how CBA for public nonmarket decision making differs from private corporate or profit-seeking decision making.
- You are able to distinguish between public and private goods in terms of nonexclusivity and nonrivalry.
- You are able to distinguish between collective and individual choice and list the limitations of CBA in dealing with this issue.
- You can set the stage for CBA by accessing data on the local demographic and economic environment.

CHAPTER 2

Cost-Benefit Analysis and Individual Preferences

It has been said that democracy is the worst form of government except all the others that have been tried.

—Sir Winston Churchill

Chapter 2 Preview

When you have completed reading this chapter you will:

- realize that market prices and surveys provide valuable information about individuals' needs and wants;
- note that cost-benefit analysis (CBA) templates list costs and benefits separately;
- understand the importance of willingness to pay (WTP) and willingness to accept (WTA) as measures of a community's valuation of goods and services;
- differentiate between cost effectiveness analysis (CEA) and CBA;
- have an intuitive understanding of conflicts and contradictions associated with what economists label "social-welfare functions" or "collective choice";
- be aware of practical difficulties associated with the adding up of preferences across households and the distribution of costs and benefits between households.

Economic Underpinnings of CBA

Unfortunately, CBA has become a generic term with no consensus on what costs and benefits should be included. In some instances, CBA is used to justify a particular project normatively without any attempt to quantify costs or benefits.[1] In this Chapter, we show that CBA need not be arbitrary, subjective, or biased in terms of public spending. CBA is not window-dressing for personal paternalistic preferences. Although it is misleading to attribute more precision to CBA than that for which it is capable, most benefits and most costs can be quantified, in local currency at current prices. Yet, CBA is merely a tool, an aid to decision-making.

Table 2.1 represents a typical template for how a particular CBA study is presented; obviously, additional information can be provided in an accompanying report.

Note that the listing of differential impacts generally differentiates groups receiving direct personal benefits from those receiving indirect public benefits. The cost listing generally differentiates on the amounts contributed by subgroups. Groups may also be broken down into low versus high income households, old versus new residents or businesses, and so forth. If an analyst for a relatively small local project decides to recognize transfers between low and high income households, a plus or minus indication could substitute for actually quantifying transfers.

We must reiterate that CBA has no usefulness unless the concepts of resource scarcity, economic efficiency, and opportunity costs are recognized. CBA assumes that individual preferences count and are revealed in market-determined prices. However, market prices are not always available or they fail to include external or social costs and benefits. In these instances, surveys and other tools are substituted to represent value that residents place on projects being considered. CBA differentiates between private and public goods, and acknowledges all the difficulties associated with public provision. It addresses as well problems associated with the aggregation of individual choice, distribution, and time preferences.

Economic Efficiency and CBA Limitations

Why is economic efficiency of any concern to those making decisions in trust for the public? To answer that question, we must understand

Table 2.1 Template for cost-benefit analysis

		Total Dollar Value (discounted)	Group 1*	Group 2*	Group 3*	Group 4*
Costs:						
	Cost a					
	Cost b					
	Cost c					
	Cost d					
	Cost e					
	Cost f					
	Cost g					
Benefits:						
	Benefit h					
	Benefit i					
	Benefit j					
	Benefit k					
	Benefit l					
	Benefit m					
Total Benefits:						
Total Cost:						
Net Benefit						

*Optional: Differential groups are identified and proposal impacts can be quantified or merely indicated with a plus or minus.

and carefully consider two types of efficiency. Economists who ascribe to Adam Smith's concept of the "invisible hand" believe that competitive private markets approximate *productive efficiency* and *allocative efficiency*. Although subservient to law, efficiency plays a role in government.

The first type of efficiency, productive or cost-minimizing efficiency, refers to producing goods and services by forgoing the least amount of alternative goods and services for any given level of benefits. The second type of efficiency, allocative or best-use efficiency, refers to using scare resources to produce whatever it is that consumers value. For example, productive efficiency is concerned that any proposed cricket pitch in

Indianapolis be built in a cost-effective manner. Allocative efficiency is concerned with assessing the value to residents or taxpayers in having a cricket pitch available for their use and enjoyment in Indianapolis.

With respect to government-provided public goods, productive efficiency is easily comprehended and generally accepted. For example, few would object to best-available technology being employed at the lowest possible cost for pothole repair or for K-12 instruction.

Allocative efficiency, however, is equally important but more difficult to comprehend. Allocative efficiency attempts to ensure that the amounts and tradeoffs between different goods and services reflect constituency values. What if very few residents of Indianapolis have any interest in a publicly proposed cricket pitch even if constructed with productive efficiency at minimum cost? To approximate allocative efficiency, CBA attempts to equate marginal cost, what the community is willing to forfeit, with marginal benefits, what the community will gain. In public education, for example, there are undoubtedly benefits to be gained from high-quality personal instruction tailored individually for each student. Unfortunately, given scarce resources there is point at which the cost of such instruction exceeds benefits. CBA assists in defining that point.

Dollar values are used to quantify costs and benefits for each relevant time period included in a particular CBA analysis. Note in Table 2.1, present values (PV) for costs and benefits are entered. When costs are incurred or benefits received, for example in the current year (2017) and in the following five years, we let $t = 0$ for 2017, $t = 1$ for 2018,.. and $t = 5$ for 2022. Then to calculate the time discounted net present value for Project x [net B], over which the decision maker has fiduciary responsibility, the discounted costs (C) of proposed Project x in each time period ($t = 0$ through n) are summed and compared with the sum of discounted benefits (B) for Project x in each time period ($t = 0$ through n). Consider the equation representing benefits (B) and costs (C) discounted over time (t):

$$\text{net B(x)} = \sum_{t=0}^{n} B_t(x)^* \, dt - \sum_{t=0}^{n} C_t(x)^* \, dt$$

Our goal is first to determine if time discounted benefits of a proposed project are positive and exceed the time discounted costs. If the net present value of benefits [net B(x)] is negative, CBA recommends that proposal x be rejected. If the net present value of benefits [net B(x)] is positive, CBA recommends that proposal x be considered (perhaps along with and compared to other projects with positive net present values).

Suppose that net benefits from the proposed Project x are positive and the decision makers decide to approve and implement Project x. Because the aim of CBA is to assess society's preferences in terms of its WTP, it follows that the decision to accept a proposal reflects the difference between the benefits obtained from a given project, say x, and the benefits that would have been obtained from private consumption or a mutually exclusive project which is foregone, say w.

$$WTP (x) - WTP (w)$$

Decision making is sequential and the complete set of alternatives at any one point in time is unknown. In other words, it is as if we were voting yea or nay on the first contestant in a beauty pageant before seeing other candidates. It is possible to solve for optimal project selection given a ranking of projects with known net benefits and a budget or borrowing constraint. However, this type of analysis is beyond the scope of this book for several reasons. First, full knowledge on the range of project options is unlikely. Second, the mathematics of solving for net benefit constrained maximization with differential weights per policy goal is frankly hazardous, too difficult, and beyond the scope of most local decision makers. Finally, we recognize and indeed insist that final screening between projects rely on some form of public choice.

In discussing rudimentary CBA, our goal is merely to deal with the binary case of one given proposal or intervention in terms of the default option of "no change," although we recognize that it is sometimes necessary to consider alternative projects having positive net present values. Consider the simple case of three projects, x (the proposed intervention), w (the default option), and z (unconsidered alternative), each with positive but different net benefits and benefit to cost ratios. Project x is preferred, if its net benefits exceed those of Project w. CBA, on the level presented in this book, is unable to offer guidance to officials entrusted with a yea or nay decision on Project x, if they are charged with addressing the likelihood of Project z, potentially offering greater net benefits.

CBA Versus CEA

Cost effective analysis (CEA), not to be confused with CBA, is a valuable tool for dealing with multiple alternatives. Suppose the policy goal is to ensure a given level of social benefits, such as a certain percentage reduction in robberies or an increase in graduation rates. CEA compares alternative means of achieving the specified goal and then considers the cost of each alternative. Note that you have already decided to "do something"; you are left to choose among a menu of alternative ways of achieving the goal. Cost effectiveness ratios can be expressed as dollars per robbery avoided or, in the case of graduation rates, the lowest dollar cost of increasing the graduation rate by 1%. Government mandates sometimes permit substituting cost effectiveness for CBA; in some cases, an agency is required to justify why CEA is the more appropriate tool.

Cost effectiveness is useful in dealing with marginal costs over a range of treatments but, unlike CBA, it lacks a calculation of benefits (because you have already decided to "do something"). In other words, CEA is useful for defining the cost of reducing, for example, certain types of pollutants by 1%, 2%, or 3% for each method under consideration. Unlike CBA, CEA does not attempt to measure the value to a community of reducing pollution by a certain amount. The economic valuation of benefits, a hallmark of CBA, provides information about residents' WTP. CBA, therefore, deals with economic efficiency because it considers resource allocation based on preferences in addition to cost minimization. CEA does neither consider nor make any attempt to insure allocative efficiency.

CBA embodies economic efficiency in three procedural steps:

1. Benefits are measured by uncovering prices consumers, donors, or taxpayers are willing to pay for a certain level of output.
2. Costs are measured at each step by supply price representing willingness to supply.
3. Costs and benefits are aggregated across individuals and groups, regardless of who within the society in question enjoys the benefit or bears the cost.

Because it attempts to go beyond simple cost-minimizing technological efficiency, CBA is rooted in the discipline of economic policy:

How much of this social good or service do residents want? How much are they willing to pay for it? As such, we need to address problems associated with aggregating preferences across a group of individuals, with considerations about who pays and who receives benefits.

CBA's Net Benefits Approach Versus Benefit Ratios

Once an analyst has summed and discounted costs (C) and (B) for a proposed project, she can solve for the benefits ratio:

$$\text{Benefits ratio} = B/C$$

The benefit ratio is a tool for eliminating worthless projects from consideration. It uses data to assess the folly of building "a bridge to nowhere." A first rule in government decision making is to eliminate projects for which the benefits ratio fails to exceed unity:

$$B/C < 1$$

However, CBA analysis does not conclude with benefit ratio analysis for two important reasons. First, multiple project proposals compete with one another. Ideally, Project x should be chosen on the basis of having higher net benefits than Project y (that is, the project that maximizes the difference between the benefits and costs):

$$\text{net } B\ (x) > \text{net } B\ (y)$$

Circumstances, on which this book is focused, are such that local decision makers are generally in the position of voting on Project x in the absence of any proposal for alternative Project y. Does this suggest, therefore, a benefit ratio test alone should be substituted for CBA's net benefit approach? Not necessarily.

This book stresses CBA's net benefit approach because the use of benefit ratios for deciding between two Projects x and y introduces a serious and significant bias. Note, carefully, that the project that maximizes the difference between benefits and cots is not the same as choosing the project that maximizes the benefit ratio!

Consider a relatively inexpensive Project (y) to provide all residents with a standardized trash bin compared to a more expensive Project (x) to deal with 100 vacant and abandoned properties. Although net benefits of Project x exceed net benefits of Project y, it is possible that the benefits ratio for Project y exceeds the benefits ratio for Project x:

$$B/C \ (y) > B/C \ (x)$$

The inconsistency between maximizing net benefits and higher benefit ratios is a matter of scale. Small projects with minuscule net benefits might have very high benefits ratios (3/2 = 1.5 compared with 25/20 = 1.25). Nevertheless, a project having the greatest net benefits (25 – 20 = 5 compared with 3 – 2 = 1) is generally preferred if the goal is to maximize net benefits with available or borrowed funds.

The rule of thumb for decision makers, then, is to use benefit ratios to eliminate worthless proposals, but be very wary of using them to choose between projects.

Does CBA Require a Social-Welfare Function?

You may recall that economists use the term social welfare to refer to the general well-being of a community. The assumption that a social-welfare function exists suggests that decision maker know how to maximize the well-being of a community by trading off benefits between individuals and by subsidizing the production of certain goods and services for others. Admittedly, CBA not only aggregates costs and benefits across individuals and groups, but it reallocates resources between private and public goods. Therefore, there is no way CBA can avoid a discussion of social-welfare functions, based on the assumption that decision makers wish to improve the overall well-being of a community.

Certainly, some analysts start with the assumption that they do indeed know what types of public goods and services could maximize the well-being of a particular community. We must be very wary about this assumption and warn against making interpersonal comparisons between costs and benefits. Can we really know if taxes harm one person less than public services benefit another? Many economists are therefore reluctant to place their confidence in any procedure that hypothesizes about theoretical benefits resulting from transferring resources from Peter to Paul or any policies designed to transfer consumption between say chocolate and broccoli.

Social-welfare theories generally engage in paternalistic judgments, implicitly accepting comparisons between one person and another. Such theories assume that decision makers know (or embody) community values and as such they can and will implement changes to improve the well-being of all residents. The mathematical modeling of some social-welfare functions is based on the diminishing marginal utility of income, a concept suggesting that an extra dollar transferred through tax dollars to lower income individuals, for example, increases total well-being. Lacking any reference to individual preferences or a WTP, social-welfare functions usually reflect the preferences of some but not necessarily those of all residents.

We wish that a social-welfare function actually existed identifying projects that would advance the well-being of the whole without inflicting harm on anyone! But such a function is not available, and it is in the nature of public goods that they be financed or subsidized through tax revenue which is coercive. Admittedly, this leaves CBA with a minor role in the collective choice process. What CBA does is provide a monetary value for direct and indirect benefits, as demonstrated by residents' behavior, either through prices of similar goods or expressed in surveys.

How does CBA assist in avoiding paternalistic judgments? It does so by using prices revealed in markets as an indicator of resident preferences. For example, if the price charged in local restaurants for a simple meal is $5, then the cost of providing a similar meal in a school lunch program should not greatly exceed this amount. Of course, it is impossible to determine the price an individual household would be willing to pay for certain services such as clean air or highways. On the other hand, differentials in property values and property taxes for similar homes in other communities can be used as a proxy representing the value households place on, for example, increased personal safety and better public schools. For cases in which a market price or a good proxy is unavailable, CBA either relies on observations of how like communities value such services or substitutes carefully crafted comprehensive surveys, samples, or simulations. Such surveys or experiments drill down to determine the likely strength of preferences associated, for example, with Options A, B, or C.

Consider Option A. Let's say that you, like many others, prefer to play golf on holidays rather than finance national celebrations that you personally take pains to avoid; Option A, prohibiting tax funding for all national holiday celebrations, is your preferred option. Option B, on the other hand, funds town celebrations for all national holiday with parades and special programs using general tax revenue. More acceptable to you personally, a well-constructed survey could reveal a clear community preference for Option C. Option C represents a WTA tax funding for one annual locally tax-subsidized national holiday celebration…as long as the celebration meets the minimum CBA benefits criterion, namely demonstrated benefits exceed costs. Your attendance at the event is not required!

Surveys represent an attempt to simulate the workings of competitive markets in situations where no such market exists.[2] When constrained by moral and legal choices, CBA is superior to alternative methods of project evaluation.[3] Used to rationally evaluate a proposal for further consideration, CBA does not necessarily presuppose assumptions about interpersonal welfare.

Michael J. Boskin, economics professor at Stanford University and former chairman of the Council of Economic Advisors, explains why economic efficiency and, hence, CBA require that net benefits be calculated in terms of all those paying costs:

> I support the federal government funding all public infrastructure projects that pass rigorous national cost-benefit tests. But here's the rub. Most federal infrastructure spending is done by sending funds to state and local governments. For highway programs, the ratio is usually 80% federal, 20% state and local. But that means every local district has an incentive to press the federal authorities to fund projects with poor national returns. We all remember Alaska's infamous "bridge to nowhere."
>
> In other words, if a local government is putting up only 20% of the funds, it needs the benefits to its own citizens to be only

21% of the total national cost. Yet every state and every locality has potential infrastructure needs that it would like the rest of the country to pay for. That leads to the misallocation of federal funds and the infrastructure projects that benefit the few at the cost of the many.

"All Aboard the Infrastructure Boondoggle," *The Wall Street Journal*, November 1, 2016, A13.

Whose preferences count? It is essential to clearly identify the standing of those from whose perspective the analysis is being conducted. If costs assumed or benefits received affect national residents, then CBA is generally done with respect to all persons living in the country. The analysis is limited to the local community, however, if no revenue is derived outside of the community from matching state or federal grants.[4]

To repeat, outside grants or fees paid by non-residents are included as CBA costs and, similarly, benefits received by outsiders must also be included. For example, both cross country travelers and local residents benefit from the same highway for which the local community receives matching state and federal grants. The basic assumption in this book is that decision makers are entrusted to act primarily on behalf of their particular constituency. However, in calculating the actual economic value of a proposal in terms of CBA net benefits, all contributions and fees from any source are considered costs and all potential benefits are included regardless of whether beneficiaries reside in and outside a local community. Of course there is nothing to preclude decision makers from doing a local analysis.

Incoherent Preferences

Individuals sometimes act inconsistently with respect to personal priorities; hence, our actions do not always reflect our long-term best interests. Researchers indicate that people often make decisions based on rules of thumb rather than strict logic. If individuals make nonrational decisions, does CBA compound these mistakes by basing decisions on misguided individual preferences or by placing too much weight on how households (perhaps mistakenly) allocate their incomes? Consider two ways in which incoherent preferences adversely affect CBA:

1. Research in Behavior Economics contributes growing evidence of incoherent preferences. For example, diners tend to purchase high-priced desserts in restaurants if sweets are presented first in a cafeteria line. Myopic employees forfeit matching employer benefits unless the match is offered as a default option on benefit forms. If individual choices are dependent simply on context and not strict rationality, this research suggests that CBA, grounded in consumer behavior, may not be in long-term public interest.

2. Can paternalistic government compensate for individual incapacity to choose wisely? Consumer sovereignty, on which CBA is based, refers to the role of consumers in directing scarce resources toward goods and services they desire. Voter sovereignty can be seen as the electorate determining who best represents their interests. Given paternalistic officials, voters can initiate proposals and hold elected officials responsible for determining the relative strength of preferences for public goods financed with tax revenue.[5]

The fundamental issue is that all methods of evaluation, including CBA and benevolent paternalistic decision-making, must acknowledge the potential for mistaken and inconsistent preferences. Officials and private individuals err in over or under allocating resources when preferences shift from revealing preferences for tennis courts at one point in time and then to skate parks or beach volleyball at another time. With CBA, at any point preferences can be simulated with simple choice experiments or with valuations revealed at the moment of consumption. This understanding of voter sovereignty is valid irrespective of whether or not these choices reveal coherent or consistent preferences.

Whenever officials assume the task of making public good decisions, the goal is to identify and realize net benefit-creating opportunities even in situations in which the market cannot be relied on to do so. For CBA to be market-simulating, rather than paternalistic, the decision maker not only rejects ineffective proposals but identifies beneficial projects for stakeholders. However, unlike a profit-seeking entrepreneur, a government official has no rights to the residual over costs and should not appropriate any surplus for him or herself. In place of the "social planner" or paternalistic agent, the market-simulation approach substitutes a "social arbitrageur." The social arbitrageur (a mythical person in CBA analysis) seeks analytically to anticipate individuals' future wants, but not to make any judgment about what is good for those individuals, or about what they would or should want if they were more rational than they really are.

Consider congestion pricing on urban roads. Observations of individuals' transport decisions are used to represent road-users' trade-offs between money outlays for road improvements and lost income due to the increased travelling time. Officials, committed to CBA, try not to impose personal value on driving more or less, but rather discern peoples' preferences at this point in time.

Distributional Considerations

CBA in its standard form takes the existing distribution of income as given. Those with larger incomes have more market votes compared to those with smaller incomes. CBA, therefore, values costs and benefits in terms of the existing distribution of income and existing property rights.

This suggests that projects benefiting low-income individuals are unlikely to gain approval as compared, for example, with publicly funded golf courses for the affluent willing to pay high user fees.[6]

In cases, presented later in this book, we will see that heavily discounted future benefits must exceed present costs for a social project to pass the minimum CBA criterion of positive net benefits. This hurdle is compounded for those projects lacking any self-generating income streams in the form of user fees. Unlike child protective service projects, for example, golf advocates can show that greens' fees provide much of the funding for public golf courses.

To address the concern that CBA places altruistic projects at a disadvantage, some analysts recommend inflating social benefits with differential weights. For example, $100 of expected playground benefits in a low-income neighborhood could be inflated with a weight of 25%, increasing the benefits to $125.

However, there are equally strong arguments for weighting costs, for all programs, to account for the fact that all taxes are coercive and affect economic behavior. There is a deadweight loss from taxpayers' response to any increase in government revenue. In other words, for every extra dollar of taxes collected, individuals strive less to earn income lowering the gross product of the area, perhaps by as much as 25%.[7]

Following through on this, higher weights on costs to adjust for marginal excess tax burden would cancel out higher weights for marginal benefits received by lower-income residents who generally pay less in taxes. Tinkering with differential weighting clouds transparency and results in perverse effects. Often, disaggregated weighting introduces a bias that serves strategic rather than economic considerations. Officials entrusted with public decision making must be aware, in reviewing outsourced CBA reports, the extent to which these reports employ differential weighing.

Differential weights for costs and benefits are probably inappropriate for rudimentary CBA in self-generated local government projects. In this book, therefore, we do not use differential weights applied to either costs or benefits.

There are three ways in which unweighted CBA self-corrects for bias in terms of the existing distribution of income. First, we carefully differentiate between public, quasi-public, and private goods, limiting CBA analysis to those goods and services having at least some public good characteristics. Second, we do not exclude human investment programs, willingly accepted by taxpayers and yielding positive long-term benefits which can be approximated. Finally, we do not assume that bureaucrats alone determine what proposals are to be evaluated. Officials and political parties are constrained by elections in which every person (regardless of income) has one vote.

Unstable Currency Values

Costs and benefits are generally measured at current prices.

Entries for each future year in the life of the project ignore inflation-indexed costs, such as mandated cost of living tuition or wage increases. Generally, we assume that this year's relative prices prevail over the life of the project. On the other hand, known or expected higher or lower real prices for specific inputs, including labor, must be estimated. For example, if fuel costs are expected to rise more or less with overall inflation, there is no need to adjust for higher fuel prices. However, if fuel prices, for whatever reason, are almost certainly expected to increase (decrease) more than general prices, then increasing (decreasing) fuel prices relative to other prices cannot be ignored.

Summary of What You Have Learned in Chapter 2

- To recognize that market prices convey information that CBA analysts use to determine individuals' preferences as revealed by their behavior in markets and expressed in appropriate surveys or simulations.
- To use WTP and WTA as criteria for indirectly revealing intensity of demand for goods and services utilizing scarce resources.
- To distinguish projects more suited to cost effectiveness analysis (CEA) than CBA.
- To outline the methodological conflicts associated with CBA as well as the assumption that paternalistic officials unfailingly operate in society's long-term interests.
- To wrestle with theoretical difficulties associated with the aggregation of preferences across households and the distribution of costs and benefits between households.
- To recognize when it is permissible to use constant prices for costs and benefits or when it is necessary to differentiate and adjust for those commodities with prices expected to deviate from the general price level.

CHAPTER 3

Time Preference and the Discount Rate

The supreme value is not the future but the present. The future is a deceitful time that always says to us, "Not yet," and thus denies us.
—Octavio Paz

Chapter 3 Preview

When you have completed reading this chapter you will:

- know how to calculate and interpret the present value of net benefits by using a procedure that discounts future costs and benefits;
- understand the reason behind discounting and the importance of choosing the appropriate discount rate;
- differentiate between ordinary observable market interest rates available to finance projects and the concept of a social discount rate;
- be attentive to assumptions associated with using different discount rates and how they can bias conclusions;
- evaluate and consider the market rate for government funds as a good approximation for a risk-free interest rate;
- be introduced to the use of sensitivity analysis in CBA.

Time Preference and the Discount Rate

County Commissioners are meeting to evaluate a proposal to build a 2-mile long railroad spur for use in a corridor of steel and energy plants within an Economic Development District. The District is generating tax revenue that could immediately be made available for development projects or, alternatively, placed in trust for the District to earn 7% in interest annually. The proposal being reviewed by the Commissioners calls for allocating a portion of these funds each year for 5 years to get the spur up and running and to pay operating costs thereafter. The Commissioners expect the County to gain benefits represented by a willingness to pay fees for using the spur and by increased income raising property values and tax revenue. There would be no resale value for the spur at the end of the 9-year time horizon following project approval.

Discounting is a method used in CBA to account for the differential timing of cost and benefits. To calculate the present value of net benefits (NPV [B]), the present value of discounted costs (GPV [C]) are subtracted from discounted benefits (GPV [B]). The concept of present value, you may recall, is also known as present discounted value. It represents a future amount of money that has been discounted because money has interest earning potential. The present value is equal to the discounted future value. With software, discounting future costs and benefits to obtain present value is relatively simple, but it is essential to know why this is done and the importance of selecting the appropriate rate for discounting future costs and benefits.

The first task in discounting is to assess the number of time periods into the future relevant for a specific project. We use the letter "t" to designate a specific time period and "n," the number of periods. In the example of the Commissioner's railroad spur there are 10 periods, with $t = 0$ to 9. The $t = 0$ period is the decision period with undiscounted initial start-up costs paid immediately.

The number of periods (n) is a judgment call depending, for the most part, on the type of project. For example, a bridge has high initial costs but the benefits extend years into the future. On the other hand, many local decisions address the "near long run" of 3 or 4 years after which a decision must be revisited. Contracts, for example, with corporations to operate municipally owned facilities are generally reviewed every few years and are thus considered "near long run" type projects.

Table 3.1, using the example of the railroad spur being considered by County Commissioners, discounts at 7% each cost and benefit by using

Table 3.1 Discounting future costs and benefits in a proposal to build a railway spur (n = 10, discount rate = 7%)

					Fiscal Year						
	2020	2021	2022	2023	2024	2025	2026	2027	2028	2029	Total
Undiscounted:											
Costs	$ (700,000.00)	$ (450,000.00)	$ (370,000.00)	$ (200,000.00)	$ (150,00000)	$ (50,000.00)	$ (50,000.00)	$ (50,000.00)	$ (50,000.00)	$ (50,000.00)	
Benefits	$ -	$ -	$ 550,000.00	$ 580,000.00	$ 1,050,000.00	$125,000.00	$ 140,000.00	$ 1,600,000.00	$1,750,000.00	$ 2,050,000.00	
	$ (700,000.00)	$ (450,000.00)	$ 180,000.00	$ 380,000.00	$ 900,000.00	$ 75,000.00	$ 90,000.00	$ 1,550,000.00	$ 1,700,000.00	$ 2,000,000.00	
Discounted:											
Costs	$ (700,000.00)	$ (420,560.75)	$ (323,172.33)	$ (163,259.58)	$ (114,434.28)	$ (35,649.31)	$ (33,317.11)	$ (31,137.49)	$ (29,100.46)	$ (27,196.69)	$ (1,877,827.98)
Benefits	$ -	$ -	$ 480,370.00	$ 473,454.00	$ 801,045.00	$ 89,125.00	$ 93,282.00	$ 996,320.00	$1,018,500.00	$ 1,114,995.00	$ 5,067,091.00
Net Benefits	$ (700,000.00)	$ (420,560.75)	$ 157,212.00	$ 310,194.00	$ 686,610.00	$ 53,475.00	$ 59,967.00	$ 965,185.00	$ 989,400.00	$ 1,087,800.00	$ 3,189,263.02
Cummulative	$ (700,000.00)	$ (1,120,560.75)	$ (963,348.75)	$ (653,154.75)	$ 33,455.25	$ 86,930.25	$ 146,897.25	$1,112,082.25	$ 2,101,482.25	$ 3,189,282.25	
Discount Factors											
Discount Rate	7.00%										
Base Year	2020										
Year Index	0	1	2	3	4	5	6	7	8	9	
Discount Factors	1	0.9346	0.8734	0.8163	0.7629	0.713	0.6663	0.6227	0.582	0.5439	

a diminishing discount factor for each year. Upfront costs of $700,000 are paid to start the project in Year 0. Note that the starting cost for Year 0 is not discounted (because the costs are paid now). All subsequent costs and benefits accrue at the end of years 1–9 (i.e., sometime in the future). In Table 3.1, we discount each cost and benefit separately based on 7% discount factors given for each year.

The purpose of Table 3.1 is to gain an understanding of discounting. Note that, aside for some rounding difference ($3,189,282 versus $3,189,263), at the end the present value of cumulative net benefits equals the NPV (B) found by subtracting GPV (C) from GPV (B). The example in Table 3.1 is unique, however, in that project funds are assumed to be available and need not be borrowed by issuing bonds; therefore, expenditures in Year 0 are not discounted. In the following chapters, we simply use a spreadsheet NPV function first to determine the GPV (C) listed as positive values and then once again to determine the GPV (B). We dispense with Year 0, and assign the first period as being Year 1 (all costs and benefits coming at the end of the year); this is consistent with the treatment found in most spreadsheets.

The advantage of using a present value formula is that the single discount rate (7% in this case) represents either the opportunity cost of earning interest on those funds or the costs of paying interest on borrowing. The choice of a discount rate is important. Note in Table 3.1 that by Year 9, given a 7% discount rate, the discount factor for costs and benefits is a hefty 54% (1,087,800/2,000,000)!

Standard practice in CBA is to report discounted costs and benefits separately. Why discount at all rather than merely adding up costs and benefits regardless of when they occur? The reason is we believe there is some rate of decline in the value of benefits received in the future rather than now and there is an opportunity cost of using funds for this project rather than for some other project. On a personal level, discounting implies that given a 5% interest rate your $100 would be able in one year to purchase goods or services selling for $105 (as opposed to those presently priced at $100). The present net benefit is $100 but the future value is $105. I am therefore indifferent between enjoying a product worth $100 now and having the choice to purchase another product a year from now for which I could pay $105.

Economists view market interest rates as revealing a society's prefer-ence for present versus future consumption. If interest rates were zero, present and future values would be mathematically equal, and future costs and benefits need not be discounted. Nevertheless, the future is uncertain, and an individual might prefer to own and use a product presently worth $100 than a better one worth $105 a year from now, even if inflation and interest rates were zero. Hence, there is a benefit to having benefits now rather than later; this concept is referred to as a positive time preference. The fact that we observe interest rates in the real world that are positive means people have revealed that they value current consumption differ-ently than future consumption; the particular magnitude of the interest rate that we see in the market gives us a good idea of the weight people place on the difference between current and future consumption.

Well-being both now and in the future is the primary economic goal. Therefore, the real costs of a project consist of consumption sacrificed today and its benefits consist of the consumption provided, directly or indirectly in the future. Communities, as well as individuals, favor pres-ent benefits over future benefits, but individuals have a single life-time horizon whereas a community may value benefits received by the next generation. Consequently, communities discount costs and benefits at a lower rate than the one observed by market interest rates. In practice, therefore, the discount rates used in CBA tend to be lower than those used for individuals and profit-seeking corporations.

Selecting the Discount Rate

Some economists suggest that using a discount rate lower than a compet-itive rate for credit in open markets misrepresents opportunity costs and favors public project expansion. The issue is whether doing so crowds out benefits from private projects which are discounted at higher rates. In other words, should we discount and thus compare the costs and benefits of a public park only in terms of the miles of road resurfacing (another public good) that could be achieved with the same borrowed government funds? Or, rather, should we discount the costs and benefits of a new park in terms of the higher nongovernment borrowing rate for a new shopping mall (a private good)?

In any case, it is standard practice to use the lower government borrowing rate to discount public projects. Doing so may imply a taxpayer-guarantee, although we have recently experienced towns in bankruptcy failing to meet their bond commitments out of general tax revenue. Generally, however, the government borrowing rate is believed to represent individuals' willingness to make risk-free loans to local governments. In addition, state and local borrowing rates are lower, given the deductibility of interest on so-called "munies" in determining federal taxes. Nevertheless, for CBA, one advantage of using the government borrowing rate is simply that it is easily observed. Also, it meets the efficiency criterion that the rate of realized benefits exceeds the cost of capital, at least in terms of the present versus the future consumption of public goods.

Should a single rate, such as the risk-free government borrowing rate, be used for discounting both costs and benefits? Public sector costs and benefits differ from those assumed and received by private individuals. Perhaps, it would be more accurate to discount private costs and benefits at a rate higher than the government borrowing rate. However, if we choose to make public or private discount modifications, a distinction must be made not only between benefits and costs which accrue to the public and those which accrue directly to individuals, but also between individuals whose net benefits are negative and those whose benefits are positive.

It would not be advisable to apply distributional weights or different discount rate to certain projects, especially if it results in ignoring results deemed unacceptable. For example, if private benefits were discounted at a higher rate, fewer social projects would meet the CBA criterion of positive net benefits. In many social programs, costs are borne publicly and benefits accrue to individuals who are private beneficiaries of public funds.

As a general rule, all costs and benefits for local projects are discounted using the risk-free government borrowing rate, with adjustments made for expected changes in the risk-free government borrowing rate. When there is a disagreement over the choice of a discount rate or when net benefits are small, refinement in the analysis is provided by using discount rate sensitivity.

Discount Rate Sensitivity

Local officials need to be acutely aware of the discount rate applied in CBA reports submitted to them for review. Different discount rates affect CBA's positive net benefit criterion.

Consider Table 3.2 in which three different rates are used to demonstrate the sensitivity of net benefits to a chosen discount rate. Suppose that Table 3.2 refers to the net benefits of purchasing a new snow plow under consideration by a town council. The plow, priced at $500,000, costs $20,000 a year to maintain and operate. These costs are due prior to the year in which the plow is used. After 3 years of use, assume that the plow no longer functions and has no scrap value. Benefits represent the value placed by residents on snow removal. If 500 highway miles are cleared on average 10 times a year, town residents, it is assumed, value snow removal at approximately $41 per mile.

Table 3.2 demonstrates two issues concerning the discounting of costs and benefits. The first, of course, is that net benefits are extremely sensitive to whatever discount rate is used. In Table 3.2, net benefits are positive approaching $20,000 if costs and benefits are discounted at a relatively low discount rate of 5%, but the same costs and benefits yield negative net benefits when discounted at the higher rate of 7%. Table 3.2 also demonstrates as well how a CBA yea or nay decision rule can favor projects yielding relatively low net benefits compared with yet unconsidered projects. When net benefits are small, it is good practice to conduct discount rate sensitivity and be open to alternatives.

At times, the concept of discounting is beyond the understanding of those interpreting a CBA report. In such instances, it is useful to simply provide a schedule of undiscounted costs and benefits. Undiscounted costs in Table 3.2 range from $520,000 in the first period down to zero in the last; undiscounted benefits range from zero in the first period to $204,630 in each of the subsequent three periods. Undiscounted costs and benefits for each period can be easily visualized in the form of a bar chart, as presented in Figure 3.1. Figure 3.1 makes no attempt to calculate net benefits; remember, it is merely an aid to visually represent the flow of costs and benefits for those unfamiliar with the concepts of discounting and present value.

Table 3.2 Three discount rates showing the sensitivity of net benefits

CBA		DR = 3%	DR = 5%	DR = 7%
Costs				
t = 0	$520,000.00			
t = 1	$20,000.00			
t = 2	$20,000.00			
t = 3	$0.00			
Total		$542,009.12	$530,655.44	$519,776.04
Benefits				
t = 0	$0.00			
t = 1	$204,630.00			
t = 2	$204,630.00			
t = 3	$204,630.00			
Total		$561,959.94	$530,722.14	$501,882.05
Net Benefits		$19,950.82	$66.70	($17,893.99)

CBA = cost-benefit analysis, dr = discount rate, t = time period.

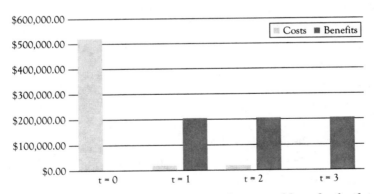

Figure 3.1 Chart comparing undiscounted costs and benefits for data used in Table 3.2

In a limited way, Figure 3.1 permits the reader to approximate positive or negative net benefits. However, this information ignores opportunity costs and risk. Therefore, discounting remains the best means of accounting for the differential timing of costs and benefits.

Summary of What You Have Learned in Chapter 3

Upon conclusion of this chapter, you should be able to:

- discount costs and benefits to adjust for differential timing;
- interpret the discount rate theoretically in terms of the time preference for present versus future consumption and in terms of the opportunity cost of loanable funds;
- outline the arguments for and against using a lower nonmarket discount rate for public projects and separate rates for public versus private costs and benefits;
- explain the advantages of using the government borrowing rate to discount costs and benefits;
- perform and interpret discount rate sensitivity calculations.

CHAPTER 4

Measuring Costs and Benefits

The language of efficiency and effectiveness is important; it appeals to the pragmatic streak inside most Americans. But it's not enough. No one is going to go to the barricades for utility.

—Samuel Gregg

Chapter 4 Preview

When you have completed reading this chapter you will:

- interpret cost benefit analysis (CBA) costs as the monetary or dollar value of alternate projects forfeited if a proposed project is implemented; for example, $80,000 spent on any project could represent one less mile of highway resurfaced;
- understand that full cost exceeds user fees, such as tolls and tuition, for publicly provided services;
- recognize that both costs and benefits are monetary values; these values represent either a willingness to accept (WTA) in terms of something undesirable, such as increased congestion, or a willingness to pay (WTP), such as the value of what must be given up to realize benefits;
- understand the role of "market failure" in creating social costs that government attempts to remediate either through regulations internalizing these costs or by direct tax expenditures; you will realize as well that markets fail in under producing goods and services with social benefits as it tends to overproduce those with social costs. When government subsidizes the consumption of goods and services containing social benefits,

beneficiaries include both the public at large and subgroups of individuals paying less than full cost;

- understand how CBA tries to account for full social costs and benefits whenever public provision compensates for market failure;
- recognize that "government failure" exists as well as market failure;
- differentiate between problems associated in quantifying costs and those associated with quantifying benefits;
- compare the use of market prices (hedonic valuation) with statistical samples and surveys (hypothetical contingent valuation) in approximating the correct quantity of certain public goods;
- identify the persons of interest, referred to as those with "standing" in a particular proposal;

The greatest challenge in CBA is assigning costs and benefits for any government project. There is a vast difference in how private firms achieve economic efficiency through competition and how government agencies operate in compensating for market failure. This is not a criticism of government agencies, but rather a recognition that they behave differently than for-profit private firms. For example, there is little correspondence between what an agency charges for a particular service and what that service costs in the first place. As such, government agencies direct their attention to all funding sources; they are less focused on users or consumers who generally pay less than full cost. Again, this is not necessarily a criticism of agencies providing public goods and services, merely a description. Public goods are provided through a collective choice process. Government agencies are attentive to officials allocating funds. It is therefore the responsibility of elected officials to advocate for residents whenever private income is reallocated from private to public spending.

To focus on residents, CBA practitioners whenever possible assign cost and benefit values based on market prices derived from the behavior of large numbers of individuals. Prices reveal valuable information useful in trying to get a handle on what residents' value and how much they are willing to pay. To ignore market prices in producing government goods and services is, consciously or subconsciously, to over or under allocate scarce resources. More importantly, it fails to take into account the revealed preferences of constituents.

Two basic CBA principles are worth repeating:

1. CBA costs are monetary values representing an opportunity foregone if a given project is approved, and
2. CBA benefits are monetary values representing the WTP either by those personally receiving benefits or as a member of the community financing them.

In this chapter, we review how private markets rely on supply and demand to approximate efficient outcomes. However, markets often fail to account for full costs and benefits. CBA is a tool used by government officials to determine if their attempts to remediate market failure accounts for all public and private costs, explicit and implicit.

Supply and Demand for Private Goods Without Social Costs or Social Benefits

There are two good reasons for reviewing supply and demand analysis at this point. First, CBA is based on the assumption that market prices provide valuable information on opportunity costs, perceived benefits, and the allocation of scarce resources. Second, supply and demand analysis is a tool for understanding why CBA is a useful or even an essential tool in determining if markets have failed by under producing goods with social benefits or by over-producing goods with harmful externalities.

In ordinary supply and demand analysis, in the absence of market failure, all costs and benefits are private. Prices are the invisible hand, so to speak, directing markets to efficiently allocate scarce resources to produce optimal quantities of private goods, such as apples and shoes. Supply curves reflect costs, and demand curves represent benefits. Figure 4.1 represents supply and demand in the market for a particular private good.

At any point to the left of Q1, resources are under-allocated, and at any point to the right of Q1 resources are over allocated.

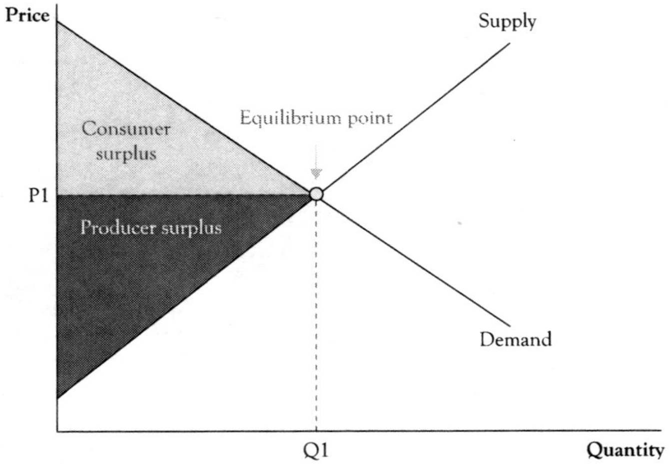

Figure 4.1 Consumer and producer surplus; at equilibrium price, firms choose not to produce more beyond equilibrium quantity (Q_1) because the extra cost of producing more exceeds equilibrium price (P_1); consumers choose not to consume beyond Q_1 because they value additional benefits less P_1

The area of maximum net benefits is the sum of consumer surplus and producer surplus. Consumer surplus is the excess of benefits over the price that consumers are willing to pay, and producer surplus refers to price in excess of the full cost to suppliers for providing a given level of output. These are real benefits that consumers and producers receive; without them, trade between consumers and producers would not take place. At the quantity associated with equilibrium price, producers choose not to produce more because beyond that output cost exceeds price. As well, consumers choose not to consume more because beyond that point the price exceeds diminishing benefits. At that equilibrium price, consumers and producers have extracted all benefits, here referred to as "surplus," available in the market.

Equilibrium price, the point at which supply and demand intersect, evolves through a market process. It is as if consumers and producers were separately conducting personal CBA-type calculation in terms of their personal goals. In fact, that is exactly what is taking place; each consumer and producer is weighing their possible actions against the costs to themselves. They make decisions by choosing what is best for them. At the intersection, as shown in Figure 4.1, the extra or marginal cost of production to the supplier is equal to the extra or marginal benefit received by the consumer. Production and consumption to the right of that point is wasteful; additional benefits are worth less than additional costs. In CBA, we are trying to determine if the optimal quantity falls to the left or right of equilibrium because ordinary market demand and supply curves ignore certain social benefits and costs. But, of course, given this failure there is no observable market to help us make the decision. That indeed is part of the reason for the existence of CBA.

In conclusion, ordinary supply and demand analysis, clearly defined ownership, profits, and competition direct markets, as if by an invisible hand, toward equilibrium. Private markets adapt to provide nutritious food, fashionable clothing, and much of whatever people need or desire. But, at times, markets fail. The term **market failure** refers to the fact that markets incorrectly allocate resources whenever actual market prices do not reflect all costs and benefits, social as well as private.

Supply and Demand with Social Costs or Social Benefits

Governments deal with market failure in three ways: *through regulating* the private sector in an attempt to force firms and households into including all costs and benefits, *through direct government provision of social goods and services,* or *through tax incentives and public financing (but not producing)* privately produced goods incorporating social benefits. Most economists, even those favoring a limited role for government, accept that in some instances markets are incapable of providing what residents need or desire. In these cases, private nonprofits or government could and should step in to fill the gap, **if and only if** the costs of doing so are less than or at least equal to the benefits.

Given market failure, officials have the responsibility to approximate optimal output. Private goods are generally produced optimally in free markets if people desire them and are willing to pay for them. On the other hand, CBA mainly deals with the production, distribution, or consumption of goods and services that involve significant social costs or social benefits, referred to as externalities. Goods and services, associated with social costs and benefits, tend to be either under, over, or not produced at all by private markets, giving rise to the term market failure.

Externalities are positive or negative effects accruing to individuals who did not choose to participate in the exchange; these are third-party effects. Externalities are sometimes referred to as spillover effects or neighborhood effects. When external or spillover effects are unpleasant because they impose costs on or reduce benefits for the public in general, they are referred to as negative externalities. For example, automobile pollution is a negative externality imposing costs, for example, on individuals with asthma. When external or spillover effects are pleasing, they are called positive externalities. For example, those inoculated for infectious diseases extend positive externalities to the public at large, including those not inoculated. Ordinary supply and demand analysis, such as that presented in Figure 4.1, can be extended to demonstrate positive and negative externalities and their effects on resource allocation.

Negative Externalities

In Figure 4.2, market supply (S_0) and demand (D_0) intersect at Point A with a price equal to $1 and an exchanged quantity of 100. In the absence of externalities and assuming perfect competition, this outcome is efficient and would be called the market equilibrium.

Suppose, however, that considerable negative externalities, such as pollution, are created in the production process harming the environment. The market price fails to reflect these negative externalities. This lowers perceived opportunity cost, encourages consumption, and over allocates resources to this good. This indicates market failure.

The negative externality of pollution can be reduced either by charging consumers more for the product or by increasing the production costs of producers. If, for example, producers are legally required to pay for environmental damages, production costs increase and the industry supply curve in Figure 4.2 shifts from S_0 to S_1. The new intersection of S_1 with D_0 at point B increases price to $1.20 and reduces output to 80 units. This outcome is preferable because without correction resources are over allocated putting the community at risk.

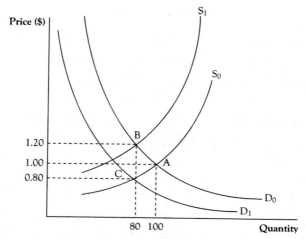

Figure 4.2 Correction for a negative externality. Requiring suppliers to internalize a negative externality shifts the supply curve to the left, moving equilibrium from A to B; the new intersection of S_1 with D_0 at Point B increases price to $1.20 and reduces output to 80 units. Alternatively, requiring demanders to internalize a negative externality shifts the demand curve to the left, moving equilibrium from A to C. The new intersection of S_0 with D_1 at Point C decreases price to $.80 and reduces output to 80 units; in both cases, equilibrium quantity decreases

Note: S = supply; D = demand.

We can also use Figure 4.2 to demonstrate correction of a negative externality by decreasing demand. Consumers, for example, generally do not take into consideration negative externalities inflicted on others from a personal decision, for example, to smoke tobacco. However, suppose that each consumer were required to have a license or pay a tax upon purchasing tobacco products. Overall demand would decrease, and D_0 would shift to D_1. As equilibrium moves from Point A to C, exchanged equilibrium quantity falls from 100 to 80.

By internalizing negative externalities into either the supply or demand curves, equilibrium quantity decreases reducing production and consumption. Point B or C is preferable to Point A in Figure 4.2, because a reduced quantity of an undesirable product is produced and consumed.

External Benefits

It is also the case that certain products have the potential of yielding positive externalities presently realized by neither producers nor consumers. Education and inoculations are but two examples. Economists sometimes use the term **merit goods** for items insufficiently produced by private markets. This is due to the market's failure to internalize positive externalities. Certain characteristics of health, education, and housing suggest that they be classified as merit goods.

Markets allocate resources insufficiently and therefore inefficiently to goods and services with positive externalities. A better allocation is achieved by either increasing the amount supplied, the amount demanded, or both. Legal or policy actions intent on increasing demand or supply will increase output and consumption.

How can policy induce suppliers to produce more? Suppliers could be subsidized for every additional unit provided. This is shown in Figure 4.3 as supply shifts to the right from S_0 to S_1. Subsidizing suppliers to internalize a positive externality shifts the supply curve to the right, moving equilibrium from A to C. The new intersection of S_1 with D_0 at point C decreases price to $.80 and increases output to 120 units.

How can policy encourage demanders to consume more? A voucher or consumer tax credit increases the demand for a good. In Figure 4.3, an increase in demand shifts the demand curve to D_1 from D_0. Encouraging demanders to internalize a positive externality shifts the demand curve to the right, moving equilibrium from A to B. The new intersection of S_0 with D_1 at Point B increases price to $1.20 and increases output to 120 units.

Either increasing supply with subsidies to producers or increasing demand with credits to consumers increases the equilibrium quantity of the good produced and consumed. Increasing supply reduces equilibrium price and increasing demand increases equilibrium price, but in both cases resources are shifted into producing more goods and services with positive externalities.

It might seem reasonable to consider negative externalities as costs, but a word of caution is in order. The reduction of a negative externality, such as pollution, is appropriately considered a benefit.

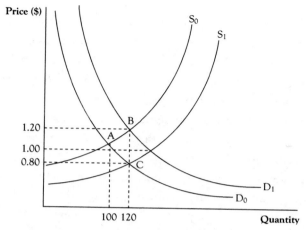

Figure 4.3 Correction for a positive externality. *Subsidizing suppliers to internalize a positive externality shifts the supply curve to the right, moving equilibrium from A to C. The new intersection of S_1 with D_0 at Point C decreases price to \$.80 and increases output to 120 units. Alternatively, encouraging demanders to internalize a positive externality shifts the demand curve to the right, moving equilibrium from A to B; the new intersection of S_0 with D_1 at point B increases price to \$1.20 and increases output to 120 units; in both cases, equilibrium quantity increases*

Note: S = supply; D = demand.

We have shown that it is theoretically possible for government to correct for market failure by attempting to adjust price and output for those goods and services with social costs or social benefits. Corrections take on many forms: regulation, subsidies, and tax incentives, as well as straight out financing and provision of public goods. In a constitutional democracy, these adjustments assume both a collective choice process and an understanding of real opportunity costs.

Caution! Government failure exits as well as market failure. Much of the distortions in market prices are not due to externalities but rather to politically-inspired government intervention in the form of tariffs, taxes, and subsidies. Corruption and cronyism are also factors. Government fails when the preferences of policy makers and interest groups are substituted for real costs and the revealed preferences of residents. CBA, based on the assumption that market prices and surveys of preferences contain valuable information, is an antidote for government failure.

Estimating Costs

In preparing a CBA, costs are generally more easily measured than benefits. That is the good news! Unfortunately, however, there is the tendency to ignore certain costs and underestimate others. Before a project is approved and implemented, policy makers must consider any uncertainties with respect to future costs. An awareness of residents' intolerance for cost or time overruns ensures that contracts be written with these contingencies in mind.

It will probably come as no surprise to learn that, even after adjusting for inflation, most CBAs err in underestimating rather than overestimating cost. In an historical sample of 258 transportation infrastructure projects, representing various types and regions, costs were underestimated about 9 out of 10 times.[1] Consistent underestimation cannot be explained by error but rather by bias on the part of project advocates.

Project promoters and decision makers are subject to moral hazard. They tend to ignore, hide, or otherwise leave out important project costs and risks in order to make total costs appear low (thus increasing the probability of acceptance of that project). The policy implications are clear. Anyone who values CBA as an appropriate tool for those acting in the public trust has an obligation to be skeptical of cost-benefit analyses produced by project promoters and their self-chosen analysts.

Competitive market costs are a good approximation in representing what a community forfeits if a project is approved. However, when markets are not competitive, the actual costs to be paid for a project exceed the true opportunity cost. Generally, however, the difference between imperfect competitive prices and opportunity costs is not material to the results. For example, compensation to credential workers generally exceeds costs if the labor markets were more open to competition, but such distinctions are beyond the scope of CBA dealing with local decision making.

Entrepreneurs, realtors, bankers, and other program advocates often receive immediate pecuniary benefits upfront for projects that fail or experience cost overruns. Cost overruns may not appear for years after project approval, long after initial advocates have moved on. Good contracts for public projects specify how the burden of cost overruns and other unforeseen adversities are to be divided between public and private interests.

The role of CBA is to list and account for all context-specific direct outlays of expenditures now and throughout the relevant time framework for the project. It must also estimate and include any external costs for which there is no market (and that is difficult). The following represents a partial list of costs that must be quantified:

- Construction costs
- Preliminary studies
- Maintenance costs
- Operating costs
- External social costs due to increased noise, congestion, and pollution
- Enforcement of regulatory compliance costs
- Private and public sector compliance costs
- Public sector costs for monitoring contract compliance
- Exhaustion of natural resources
- Foregone tax revenue

Measurement of Benefits

Benefits, as compared with costs, are more difficult to identify and measure. However, the process alone of identifying and listing benefits is worthwhile. This process helps in eliminating double-counting and in ranking benefits in order of significance. Comparing these lists with similar projects in other localities is invaluable. The key is having a clear understanding of what constitutes benefits and for whom.

Consider a proposed state program to jump-start economic development in rural areas. If approved, the state extends a total of $150 million over the next 3 years for grants and administrative expenses to foster new rural businesses; in addition, the state guarantees bonds issued by qualifying firms. These firms are eligible as well for tax credits equaling $210 million over the next 10 years. Realize that tax credits are considered tax expenditures and therefore represent costs to the state. We assume that the state insures against bond default. The present value of the proposed state development program costs is $314 million as estimated in Table 4.1.

Table 4.1 CBA for a hypothetical proposed state program to create jobs in rural areas (discount rate: 5%, Dollar in millions).

Year	1	2	3	4	5	6	7	8	9	10	PV
Costs:											
Administrative	$ 0.5	$ 0.5	$ 0.5	$ 0.5	$ 0.5	$ 0.5	$ 0.5	$ 0.5	$ 0.5	$ 0.5	($ 3.9)
State Grants to Business	$ 50.0	$ 50.0	$ 50.0								($ 136.2)
Bond Default Insurance	$ 1.50	$ 1.50	$ 1.50	$ 1.50	$ 1.50	$ 1.50	$ 1.50	$ 1.50	$ 1.50	$ 1.50	($ 11.6)
Tax Credits	$ 21.0	$ 21.0	$ 21.0	$ 21.0	$ 21.0	$ 21.0	$ 21.0	$ 21.0	$ 21.0	$ 21.0	($ 162.2)
PV of Costs:											($ 313.8)
Benefits:											
Wages*		$ 14.00	$ 28.00	$ 28.00	$ 28.00	$ 28.00	$ 28.00	$ 28.00	$ 23.00	$ 28.00	$ 176.84
PV of Benefits:											$ 176.84
Net Benefits:											($ 136.92)

* If $28 million in annual wages for this proposal were extended annually through Year 21, the present value of wages would be $320.

CBA = Cost benefit analysis; PV = Present value.

What are the potential benefits to state residents? It is estimated that 250 permanent jobs paying $70,000 annually are created in the year following approval increasing to a total of 500 jobs the following year. What does this mean for CBA benefits from an economic point of view? If 10% of the newly employed travel to their job but reside in another state and another 10% of employees transfer from existing jobs, total jobs created by the program must be adjusted downward. We will use an annual wage of $70,000 estimate for quality of life benefits accruing to any previously unemployed resident. This assumes that federal taxes paid on this gross income are reallocated back to the state. Realize that the use of full wages as benefits implies zero value from leisure or household consumption for unemployed workers. Table 4.1 estimates the present value of these benefits at approximately $177 million.

Clearly the example as given in Table 4.1 does not satisfy the CBA criterion hurdle for positive net benefits. Did we neglect to list all the various types of benefits? The note in Table 4.1 suggests positive net benefits at the end of 21 years, but there is no guarantee that the firms will not automate (thus reducing employment), relocate, or both. If new businesses are owned and financed out of state, profits and interest payments do not represent in-state benefits. Newly employed workers contribute to state tax revenue, but these amounts are included as part of gross wages. State businesses may experience increased revenue, but these amounts are likewise included in gross wages. Certainly, the morale and aesthetics of the community are important but these effects are probably due to increased disposable income, not additions to well-being. Finally, it is unlikely that a single program would result in a long-term stimulatory impact on growth in the state's gross product.

It is, however, legitimate for the example presented in Table 4.1 to estimate benefits to state residents in general by offering jobs to the previously unemployed. On a state level, the reduction in crime due to the program is probably insignificant. On the other hand, any reduction due to the program in existing state welfare or unemployment payments is clearly a CBA benefit to residents in general.

If the present value of net benefits (NPV [B]), including benefits presently omitted from Table 4.1, exceeds $136.92 million, the analyst, even if the program is contrary to his or her political philosophy, must conclude and clearly state that benefits exceed costs (and the project should be considered). With negative net benefits, as presented in Table 4.2, a decision maker can make the public aware of the cost per state resident of the program. Or, given the data, calculate that each new job created by the program has a present value of $320,000! Decision makers could choose to calculate and report subsidies per state resident. However, the analyst should recommend that the project be rejected based on simple, unmodified CBA guidelines.

In the previous hypothetical example, market wages, rather than the change in wages, are used as a measure of benefits. This simplification implies that additional quantities of certain types of labor, goods, and services are available at the same wage or price. Total benefits, in other words, are in some CBAs expressed simply as price (or wage) multiplied by quantity. The constant price (or wage) assumption assumes a horizontal supply curve and ignores producer surplus. Such modifications from the theoretically optimal assumptions can be explicitly stated in the CBA report.

Generally, a proposal subsidizing supply lowers price for an existing good or service. Given consumer surplus as defined in Figure 4.1, additional benefits accruing from a new project, such as a municipal swimming pool, would be the change in the local price of entrance to swimming pools times the change in the number of users. In practice, we often substitute the lower price (rather than change in price) multiplied by the change in output to estimate benefits.

CBA benefits represent valuations as revealed by actual behavior. Consider people parking closer to their destination for a fee of 50 cents rather than walking 5 minutes more from a parking space further away. In this way, drivers have revealed that their time is worth more than 10 cents per minute. A CBA analyst, in this case, can extend the 10 cents per minute value in quantifying benefits for other time-saving projects. The point is that CBA requires surveys that quantify what people do, would choose to do, and either are WTP or WTA, not simply goods and services for which they express a desire.

In dealing with goods not traded in private markets, the challenge is to identify a dollar WTP for those actually receiving benefits as well as those taxed to subsidize provision. User fees and quality of life measures are used for direct beneficiaries. However, preference surveys and other indirect means must be used to determine willingness to subsidize projects for which certain residents receive no direct benefits. The indirect benefits to nonusers of public goods are referred to as **existence values**.

WTP, at the margin, is the extra amount of money a resident or user would give up to have an additional unit of a good produced. WTA, at the margin, is the extra amount a resident or user would pay to avoid an additional unit of something unpleasant. For simplification, we use the term WTP interchangeably to represent the value of preferred items increased or undesired items decreased.

The following is a partial list of the types of CBA benefits quantified in dollar values:

- Lives saved
- Time saved
- Accidents avoided
- Reduced noise, congestion, and pollution
- Additional tax revenue
- Increases in private consumption
- Improvements in health
- Scrap value at end of project
- User fee revenue
- Net increase in property values
- Crime reduction

Using Surveys to Assess Willingness to Pay or Willingness to Accept

Let's review three methods commonly used for valuing costs and benefits. In the first, the researcher paternalistically assigns a "judgment value." In the second and preferred method, market prices based on the behavior of consumers and firms are used. Prices, determined through competition in the market, are assumed to represent the cost to firms in providing a good and the value consumers place on its benefits. Such valuations are referred to as hedonic valuations. In hedonic valuation, CBA avoids paternalism and instead focuses on behavior-revealing preferences ("Don't ask people what they want, instead watch their behavior"). Finally, in the absence of markets revealing preferences for public goods, CBA relies on surveys and samples as a substitute for observed behavior to assess WTP. These valuations are referred to as hypothetical contingent valuations.

Surveys including all residents or random samples elicit preferences using hypothetical questions. They are less revealing than direct observation of behavior because they are based on self-reporting preferences. Survey answers often represent strategic self-serving behavior. Or, respondents might simply enjoy expressing support for what they perceive as a good cause.

Survey information is often biased because respondents have little incentive to be truthful or to formulate carefully reasoned responses. In particular, there is a natural tendency to strongly state preferences for desirable goods in the absence of cost considerations. Better questions avoid a narrow framing of preferences such as, "How much would you benefit if proposal X were approved?" Drilling down to uncover a willingness to trade-off options is achieved when surveys present bundles of attributes from which to choose: closer parking, safer parking, close and safer parking, lower taxes, and so forth.

Although they do not approach the quality of behavioral hedonic valuations, statistical surveys have become more sophisticated. A good survey contains questions emphasizing how project costs are to be paid. A survey of all residents is ideal but generally cost prohibitive. Therefore, random samples are taken of those with standing in the decision; CBA then extends these results to the total population.[2]

Sample questions and answers refer to monetary values or opportunity costs in terms of WTP. WTP for something desirable, such as clean air, can be equated as previously noted to WTA something undesirable, such as having to pay for clean air or having to tolerate a certain level of pollution. However, practitioners find WTA terminology useful in framing survey questions.

Many studies report higher WTP support when respondents have the option of answering yes or no to a particular proposal with a fixed cost; therefore, a range of costs increases accuracy in estimating WTP. On the other hand, when presented with a range of costs, respondents are influenced by the starting figure. "Framing" the question is often as important as the question itself. It may be necessary to design several survey copies with different ranges and randomly assign respondents across slightly different surveys.[3]

Sequential sampling of the same residents can be used to rule out inconsistent revealing of preferences in determining, for example, if a community pool is definitely preferred to a skate park versus a tennis court. This type of sampling is particularly suited to small municipal projects for goods that are not available in markets with competitive prices. Surveys and samples are expensive to conduct, and at times officials understandably adapt surveys based on populations similar to local residents.

CBA is an information gathering process. Simulations and big data statistical methods supplement information on how residents value benefits. In these cases, calibrated choice experiments simulating real-life situations are used to observe selection behavior. Finally, analytics, regression analysis, and alternatives to direct surveys use large databases to study prices, attributes, and associated values for certain amenities such as safety and commute times.

Whose Benefits and Whose Costs Count?

CBA has relevance only when limited to a particular constituency. The identification of standing is critical in deciding which and whose costs and benefits are relevant. A CBA with a global perspective, for example, incorporates pollution costs affecting anyone regardless of where he or she resides on the planet. On the other hand, a statewide perspective considers how a proposed new university affects enrollment at other universities elsewhere in the state, but not necessarily enrollment at universities in other states.

The identification of constituency is an important issue in fiscal federalism, in which tax revenue is believed to be more effectively collected centrally and then redistributed to local government units. Fiscal federalism is intended to provide local choice and discretion, but often comes in the form of matching funds if and only if local government units agree to implement certain programs.

Consider a proposal to build sewers co-financed by property owners, the city, the county, and the state. If state or federal funds match or subsidize local projects, there is a tendency to assess costs and benefits, public and private, exclusively in terms of local residents. Local officials pay a political price if perceived as "leaving free money on the table." Yet, some officials are willing to pay this price for two good reasons. Either, they object to projects yielding negative net benefits when costs to all taxpayers are included. Or, they recognize CBA limitations in determining if matched funds redirect local tax dollars to less beneficial projects.

The focus of this text is local projects. Therefore, decision makers are acting in trust on behalf of local residents. Undeniably, better managed communities compete with each other to retain and attract firms and households. However, CBA is not intended as a strategic tool to "beggar thy neighbor." The CBA goal is neither to shift costs onto neighboring communities nor to reap benefits at their expense. There is a strong case to be made for block grants awarded by state and federal government to be used for a variety of projects selected by local governments. Block grants more clearly identify the opportunity cost in terms of forfeited opportunities when approval is granted for a particular project partially financed with state and federal funds.

Timing of CBA

A local Council considers a proposal to build a three-bay firehouse with additional room for borough offices and meetings. The Council President independently presents the motion to approve an expenditure of $28,000 to pay for a preliminary architectural, structural and mechanical plan to be drawn up. Does approval of this motion put the cart before the horse?

Revenue to cover costs of the proposed firehouse, office, or meeting facility is expected to consist of some combination of a low-interest state loan, private donations, contributions from the county fire department, a recently adopted local service tax, and, if necessary, a bank loan. The Council President argues that the current firehouse needs upgrading to keep pace with growing fire protection technology and that urgent action is needed to advance this project. The President argues that a $28,000 commitment is reasonable to determine feasibility of the project.

Legitimate issues are feasibility, appropriateness, and the scope of any proposal evaluated both in terms of whose interests are being served and a consensus on what constitutes the acceptance criterion. CBA attempts to answer these questions. Without addressing efficiency in terms of WTP for valued services, feasibility studies at best offer only technological cost effectiveness. Local residents would be better served by a preliminary but comprehensive CBA, starting with feasibility, to implementation, through completion, given an appropriate present value framework for such a project.

In the initial appraisal stage, when officials must vote yea or nay, the potential for error is recognized. Certain impacts are inevitably and inadvertently omitted from the analysis; forecasting and measurement are imprecise to say the least. Ongoing analysis and adjustments are required. Throughout the decision process and implementation, it is prudent to reassess and decide if certain projects should be modified or terminated. For full transparency, ex-post studies can be used to identify mistaken assumptions and errors in previous CBA analysis.

An advocate of CBA is not suggesting that assured definitive economic efficiency be the sole criterion for local government decisions. It is merely suggesting that efficiency and rational choice be part of the process from the beginning.

Summary of What You Have Learned in Chapter 4

Upon conclusion of this chapter, you should be able to:

- use supply and demand analysis to explain how competitive markets in the absence of market failure optimally allocate resources in providing private goods;
- then, extend supply and demand analysis to incorporate positive and negative externalities as social costs and benefits that markets fail to internalize;
- show how laws, regulations, subsidies, taxes, and direct government provision of public goods shift ordinary supply and demand to nudge output in a desired direction;
- outline arguments showing why, in practice, CBA costs tend to be underestimated and why benefits are more difficult to quantify;

- explain why hedonic valuations based on behavior is the preferred means of assessing costs and benefits;
- explain the use and limitations of samples and surveys using hypothetical contingent valuations in those instances when markets for public goods do not exist;
- clarify the standing of certain groups in CBA decision making.

CHAPTER 5

Shadow Pricing

To press non-economic values into the framework of the economic calculus, economists use the method of cost/benefit analysis...it is a procedure by which the higher is reduced to the level of the lower and the priceless is given a price. It can therefore never serve to clarify the situation and lead to an enlightened decision. All it can do is lead to self-deception or the deception of others; for to undertake to measure the immeasurable is absurd and constitutes but an elaborate method of moving from preconceived notions to forgone conclusions....
—E. F. Schumacher (1973)

Chapter 5 Preview

When you have completed reading this chapter you will:

- realize that market values for certain costs and benefits are not always available; this is, particularly, the case for intangible quality of life services;
- understand that, when market prices are unavailable for costs or benefits, shadow prices, based on residents' behavior, are used as substitutes;
- evaluate a shadow price for lives saved as one example of a proxy used to avoid assessing benefits arbitrarily;
- know when it is best to substitute cost effective methodology in place of CBA's monetary valuations;
- consider the unique role shadow prices play in measuring willingness to pay or willingness to accept;
- begin to understand how CBA analysts proceed cautiously to place monetary values on what many consider nonquantifiable costs and benefits.

Consider a corporate team deciding whether or not to purchase a new piece of equipment. The initial cost of the machine and operating costs are known. If anyone is willing to purchase at full price whatever good or service that can now be produced with this new piece of equipment, the revenue generated over the life of the machine is compared with the cost of purchasing the machine. The decision to follow through with the purchase is straightforward, whenever the present value of revenue exceeds the present value of costs.

Compare the corporate decision making described earlier with a public or joint public-private decision to initiate a drug rehabilitation program. In such a program, there are social benefits accruing to residents in general as well as private benefits to clients. Multiple funding sources include repurposed staff and facilities, client fees, tax revenue, grants, and donations. CBA's task is to determine if the sum of private and social benefits, extremely challenging to assess, exceeds the sum of explicit and implicit costs. Shadow prices are needed to measure benefits generated for resources allocated toward this and similar projects.

The benefit of a drug rehabilitation program, for example, can be thought to equal the present value of a drug-free year multiplied by total years achieved by participating clients. But what is the value of a drug free year? Initially, we need to identify whatever it is that program sponsors are attempting to optimize: potential client earnings, quality of life for each participant, reduction in crime and dependency, improved health and extended life, humanitarian considerations, and so forth. Realistically, local decision makers do not calculate marginal benefits for each of these goals, but, nevertheless, rational decision making requires an attempt to measure and quantify outcomes.

In rudimentary cost benefit analysis (CBA), **shadow price** is a general term referring to estimates used as substitutes for market prices. To say that intangibles cannot be precisely valued is not to say that trade-offs cannot be considered logically. Shadow prices are not real prices in that they are not listed anywhere and are not directly observed in a market, but, given that resources are limited, they represent an attempt to approximate opportunities foregone, the value of goods and services sacrificed in order to obtain another good or service.

The absence of a direct market for the public goods, does not imply that residents' preferences and valuations be ignored. There are surrogate markets for determining valuations. For example, wage differentials between jobs that vary in risk of personal injury indicate the value that individuals in the community place on personal safety and their degree of risk aversion. Similarly, there is no market for noise abatement. However, the market price for a house near an airport and subject to jet noise is generally lower than the price of a similar house in a quieter neighborhood. These differences provide information on the value residents place in avoiding undesirable outcomes.

In some instances, actual market prices are good substitutes for shadow prices. For example, the shadow price for a public school lunch may be valued at the price found in the market for a comparable meal at a private restaurant. Of course, analysts must consider if present prices really do reflect the marginal cost of producing the good if markets are not competitive, experience scale considerations, or are subsidized. However, such market distortions are minor compared with those associated with arbitrarily placing values on social outcomes as benefits.[1] Fortunately, once actual benefits and costs are clearly identified, market price proxies for shadow prices are often available.

Shadow Prices When Comparable Market Prices Are Not Available

The "willingness to pay" method for the difficult task of determining a shadow price for the value of human life is based on observation. It measures the desire of individuals to extend their lives by how they allocate their incomes. This value can be used to evaluate proposals known to reduce the likelihood of dying. For example, by ordering optional side-impact airbags on a new automobile, individuals gain a small reduction in the probability of dying. A market price above which most residents are willing to forgo optional side airbags represents the value placed on reducing a known probability of dying. CBA can use this monetary value to compare the benefits of decreased traffic deaths with the costs of installing guard rails on dangerous curves on public highways.

Individuals signal their WTP to achieve longer expected lives by purchasing airbags. Suppose the reduced probability of dying in a car accident with or without side airbags is P and the cost of the airbags is C. Individuals purchase safety devices up to the point at which the perceived benefit is zero. Therefore, we solve for the value residents place on a person's life (V) based on their WTP the cost of airbags.

$$P * V = C$$
$$V = C/P$$

If, for example, most residents forfeit purchasing a safety device costing $3,000 (C) with a known probability of reducing death per automobile by 0.005 (P), they indicate that the value to them of a life saved is about $600,000 (V).

We do not intend to appear sanguine about quantifying lives lost or saved. A specific person, or a number of specific persons, is not designated in advance as the individual saved or killed if a particular project is undertaken. Given a community's behavior in avoiding risk, the benefits gained (lost) do not award (compensate) a specific number of persons for their lives (deaths) but rather award (compensate) each person in the community for the decreased (additional) risk to which he or she is to be exposed. Any decreased or increased risk of death, associated with a proposed project, is included in CBA as one of a number of economic consequences all of which affect the well-being of each member of the community.[2]

Placing values on what many consider nonquantitative costs and benefits raises a legitimate concern about false accuracy, but consider the following analogy. Suppose I agree to sell the home of my childhood at market price. The selling price does not represent my greater intrinsic or personal value. The decision to sell at market price merely indicates that the instrumental value of selling outweighs the intrinsic value of keeping the property, given present circumstances. In the public realm, shadow prices attempt to mimic the trade-offs current residents are making between costs and benefits.

The legitimacy of using "shadow prices" depends on how precisely an analyst can pin down those values. Analysts should not suspend judgment by accepting poor shadow prices for the sake of quantifying costs and benefits. Operating in a professional manner, the analyst should be reasonably certain that these values lie within a range of 10% to 20% of what the actual values may be, or even 30% of what is thought to be reasonable and accurate. Otherwise, the analyst can refuse to submit a CBA report and simply pass the decision back to the responsible public official. There is a range of projects over which the ability of analysts to quantify benefits and costs is too limited and too vague for CBA to contribute value to the decision-making process.[3]

Each project proposal presented to a decision maker offers a unique challenge. Before proceeding, researching CBA reports and case studies for like-projects in similar localities is strongly recommended. With necessary modifications, available shadow prices can substitute for creating new ones, avoid costly superficial samples and surveys, or both. The typology, presented in Table 5.1, is not exhaustive but represents a way to start thinking about market *versus* shadow prices for certain types of projects.

Any system can be gamed and CBA is no exception. For example, consider an official advocating taxes to reduce a negative externality such as carbon emissions. If a proposed tax of one million dollars were expected to reduce carbon emissions annually by 10 tons, then the analyst, in order to guarantee approval, could inappropriately suggest that the shadow benefit to a society for a ton of carbon emissions was $100,000. Shadow prices for costs and benefits must be independently established.

At times, user fees for government provided services coincide with direct benefits to clients or third parties paying full cost. In such cases, CBA reduces to financial analysis. However, for most public-sector projects, decisions must be made when direct beneficiaries do not pay full cost. For effective governance, shadow prices are needed to correctly and fully account for direct and indirect costs and benefits. Critics of CBA maintain that the attempt to quantify immeasurable values is delusional and dangerous. No doubt this is the case for certain human experiences. We maintain, however, that shadow pricing is a legitimate tool for assessing valuation revealed either by behavioral choice or by willingness to pay surveys of those for whom decision-makers act in trust. CBA makes no claim to produce morally correct decisions; it is not a substitute for rule of law, good governance, or public choice.

Avoiding Shadow Prices

Benefits, such as those resulting from protecting an endangered species, are difficult to quantify. Therefore, we need to determine the total amount

Table 5.1 Potential market vs. shadow price valuations for costs and benefits by project type

Project type	Transportation and infrastructure	Environment and natural resources	Social: Health, education, recreational, welfare
When market prices are available for valuing either costs or benefits:	Use actual market prices of land, labor, equipment, and maintenance costs for construction and maintenance costs.	Use actual market prices of land, labor, equipment, and maintenance costs for construction and maintenance costs.	Use actual market prices for staff and facility costs.
	Assess benefits in terms of actual cost savings and the market value of outputs.	Assess benefits in terms of actual cost savings and the market value of outputs.	Assess benefits at actual prices paid for similar goods and services in the private sector.
When shadow prices need to be chosen and substituted for valuing costs or benefits:	Evaluate monetarily the lives saved, time saved, injuries reduced, and accidents avoided.	Estimate the loss of output or income due to additional regulations.	Estimate the cost of any loss of output or income due to increased taxes.
	Measure willingness to pay for similar air quality, noise reduction, and aesthetic or property improvements.	Measure willingness to pay for similar air quality, noise reduction, and aesthetic or property improvements.	For benefits substitute increased lifetime income due to educational, productivity, and health improvements.
			Substitute decreased home insurance costs as a benefit of crime reduction.
	Outsourced costs and benefits may be substituted for assessing internal costs and benefits.	Outsourced costs and benefits may be substituted for assessing internal costs and benefits.	Outsourced costs and benefits may be substituted for assessing internal costs and benefits.

Source: Based on Boardman et al. (1997).

of funds the public is willing to reallocate from equally valued endeavors. To avoid the expense of such a study, analysts often adopt a cost-effective methodology to compare, for example, different means of species preservation for a given expenditure level. For this purpose, cost-effective methodology may be preferred to CBA. Federal agencies, required by law to perform CBA, are sometimes permitted to substitute cost effectiveness analysis (CEA) when justified in terms of specific mission.

CEA has the additional advantage of not having to translate costs and benefits into monetary units. For example, in health care policy, CEA can use quality adjusted life-years (QALY) rather than monetary values. Nevertheless, CBA is the preferred methodology if the goal is to compare decreasing additional benefits with increasing marginal costs.

Risk and Uncertainty

It is impossible to guarantee precision in CBA calculations given contingencies affecting costs or benefits in the near and long term. In is tempting, therefore, for an analyst to adjust expected net benefits for risk. Although risk adjustment is mathematically straightforward, there are several good reasons for not following through on risk adjustments.

CBA is a tool, given present information, to eliminate error implicit in someone's hunches about net benefits. Each local project is unique, unlike actuarial-type forecasting based on group experience. The CBA decision rule uses market and shadow prices to determine if benefits exceed costs, not to propose a range into which net benefits are likely to fall.

In policy deliberation, CBA is a process for acquiring information. If we admit to imprecision in calculating net benefits, what is this information worth? Suppose that CBA reduces error by approximately a quarter of net project value. Assume this reduction is worth, according to one study, at least 2% of mean net benefits of appraised projects.[4] Translation: If in one term as a local decision maker, you evaluate projects yielding on average $200,000 in net benefits. Given 50 hours of your time for each CBA calculated, the shadow price of your time is $80 per hour. Warning: Do not expect to be fully compensated as a local government official!

Summary of What You Have Learned in Chapter 5

Upon conclusion of this chapter, you should be able to:

- use shadow prices as proxies when market prices are unavailable;
- proceed cautiously to place monetary values on what many consider nonquantitative costs and benefits, such as years of life and time saved;
- start CBA analysis by clearly listing all costs and benefits and proceed to research the availability of market, shadow price, or both valuations;
- outline arguments showing when CEA versus CBA is more appropriate;
- explain in terms of hedonic *versus* contingent valuation why surveys may not reveal the willingness to pay or willingness to accept criteria of CBA;
- explain how a person signals his or her willingness to pay to achieve extended life in terms of the following: $P * V = C$ and $V = C/P$;
- clarify the use of market, shadow prices, or both based on project type;
- exercise personal judgment on the selection and use of shadow prices.

Potential Pitfalls in Cost Benefit Analysis

The curious task of economics is to demonstrate to men how little they know about what they imagine they can design.

—F. A. Hayek

Chapter 6 Preview

When you have completed reading this chapter you will:

- realize why cost benefit analysis (CBA) uses marginal benefits and marginal costs. The word marginal is used here to mean the "change in benefits" or "change in costs" for the project being considered;
- understand that in certain instances assignment of dollar values as either a cost or benefit, does not affect net benefits; reduced delinquency, for example, can be viewed by one analyst as a benefit and by another as contributing to cost reduction;
- be warned that the piling on of dubious benefits is unacceptable;
- understand that wages in general are costs not benefits; workers and volunteers have opportunity costs; CBA does not consider residents merely as job holders or source of tax revenue;
- know the important role that user fees play but realize that they generally do not represent full cost;
- accept that CBA uses simplifying assumptions about linearity in calculating costs and benefits.

Potential Pitfalls in Cost Benefit Analysis

Obviously, it makes little economic sense to outsource a CBA costing $500,000 for a proposal costing little more than $500,000 to implement. There is no reason, however, why local decision makers cannot take it on themselves to perform rudimentary nonprofessional CBA for certain projects. In fact, it should be encouraged. That is the very reason this book has been written. In this section, we outline pitfalls, hazardous to analysts, professionals, and nonprofessionals. We do this mindful of this book's fundamental limitations, namely the brevity of presentation and the unbounded scope of government projects.

CBA is both an art and a science. It demonstrates well two economic sayings: first, "Anything worth doing is worth doing poorly," and, second, "Do not let the best be enemy of the good." CBA limitations are recognized, but some of its most severe weaknesses are known and apparent prior to project acceptance and implementation.

Limitations and Complexity

We are familiar with officials whose primary goal is to grow the local economy solely in order to maximize tax revenue. At best, his or her perception of leadership is to use tax revenue to create communities reflecting a personal vision. This is the antithesis of CBA, attempting to discern what residents value. Of course, it is essential that those preparing a CBA not be directly associated with private interests associated with the project. This is particularly difficult to achieve in small towns. CBA's "with project or without project" comparisons along with officials who are realistic about priorities and the scope of local government assist in maintaining a degree of objectivity.[1]

Economic income distributional policies and stabilization interventions are in general conducted on the federal level. Because CBA in this text deals with local proposals, the focus is on accounting for private and external costs and benefits to minimize waste and improve economic efficiency.

One key in avoiding common CBA pitfalls is to focus on marginal economics, comparing additional benefits gained with additional costs. For example, the 10th bridge over a local river yields less benefits than the 9th and this is represented by a downward movement along the demand curve to a lower willingness to pay. The price that people are willing to pay equals the extra benefit received (in fact, another name for a demand curve is the marginal benefits curve). Similarly, higher costs for constructing the 10th bridge compared to the 9th is represented by a movement upward along the supply curve. Higher prices are necessary to increase supply if firms have to woo labor and inputs from other sectors by paying higher compensation. The socially optimal number of bridges is achieved when the benefits enjoyed by the community of the last bridge equals the extra costs of construction and maintenance.

Procedural Differences

One analyst may be inclined to net certain costs out of a particular benefit and another analyst may be inclined to net certain benefits out of a particular cost. For example, consider a CBA park proposal in which improved recreational opportunities for all is the primary goal. One analyst may treat less delinquency as a benefit measured in terms of reduced patrolling costs. Another analyst may reduce increased patrolling costs to account for reduced delinquency. This is not a serious problem, although it does affect benefit or cost ratios. Such differences will **not** raise the benefit cost ratio above one if the ratio is less than one and overall net benefits remain the same.

Exaggerating Benefits and Overstating Multiplier Effects

Over- and under-assignment of costs and benefits are serious CBA problems. In particular, the piling on of dubious benefits, such as those transmitted to future generations, are often used to "sell" projects to the general public. Therefore, benefits that are uncertain, unquantifiable, and immaterial are misleading and should be excluded from the analysis.

Economists, even those of the Keynesian persuasion, cringe as CBA studies revert to pseudo-multiplier analysis and impact studies. Small local projects are unlikely to pump up aggregate demand creating prosperity, economic growth, and jobs. One shot increases in spending financed from tax revenue, with municipal debt, or both do not represent a sustained exogenous increment shifting aggregate expenditures up toward a new equilibrium. They will not propel the whole region onto a higher growth path. Generally, local projects are not associated with significant macroeconomic aggregate income effects. Two possible exceptions may occur either when the marginal propensity to spend on housing is large or when wage income is substituted for leisure increasing labor supply.[2]

Consider a proposal to expand an early childhood intervention program. To determine benefits, at first glance it appears reasonable to compare the lifetime yearly earnings of a program participant with the earnings of a nonparticipating individual. However, this type of project is an intermediate good and, therefore, accounts for only a part of any boost in lifetime earnings. Life-long increased earnings of participants should be adjusted down to account for subsequent interventions. On the other hand, if the program actually provides, in addition to human investment effects, recreational and child-care components, the income comparison method underestimates program benefits. The price that local parents are willing to pay for similar early childhood programs is a valid proxy for per child benefits. This value, transparent and observable, bundles daycare with education, and is a good base on which to begin the analysis.

User Fees

User fees are charges paid out-of-pocket for licensing, permits, parking, health testing, housing while incarcerated, and other government service. They are not market prices (because they are not determined in a market, they are usually set by an agency official), and range from 0% to 100% of full costs associated with providing the service. Recipients of poverty and refugee services, for example, pay little or no fees but municipally owned utilities, toll bridges, and controlled access highways charge close to full cost (and sometimes more than full cost).

The downside of user fees for subsidized goods and services is that inevitably quantity demanded exceeds optimal output. Efficient optimal output is defined as the quantity at which marginal cost equals marginal benefits. Public goods, when subsidized, are perceived as a bargain because one does not pay full cost. Students, for example, may be inclined to extend the number of semesters needed to complete their studies. An exception to the generalization of overconsumption exits when user fees operate to exclude low-income taxpaying households. Grounds fees at municipal golf courses and tuition at state universities are two examples.

The attractive upside of user fees is that they make government agencies more responsive to clients. Furthermore, fees ration goods and services to those somewhat WTP out-of-pocket. User fees help to create a quasi-market when ordinary markets do not exist. Entrance fees to national parks are one example. An analyst must determine if the number of entrances multiplied by the fee charged approximates the value of user benefits. For national parks, it is likely that marginal benefits for visitors are positive but less than the marginal cost of providing the service. Additional benefits may accrue to nonusers who never visit a local park, museum, or library yet nevertheless experience satisfaction knowing that such services are available. These indirect benefits, referred to as "existence values," are appropriately assessed along with direct user benefits.

Transfers

CBA is all about transfers, transfers between types of goods and services provided by local government and transfers between private and public consumption. The goal is to increase the well-being of residents and to maintain or increase overall quality of life. The primary focus of CBA is not to redistribute income and wealth between households. However, most government programs have the effect of transferring income between households.

Proposals are often justified in terms of reducing the income of the affluent in order to transfer benefits to low-income households. The actual effect is often to redirect resources between subsets of interest groups. At least in the short run on a local level, transfers to equalize income are relatively insignificant. Although local CBA reports may explicitly identify the direction of transfers between residents, we neither recommend income redistribution be pursued as a primary goal of local government nor recommend quantifying it as a benefit.

Wages Represent Costs Not Benefits

The CBA assumption is that resources for proposed projects are necessarily reallocated away from producing other goods and services; these funds have an alternative use, an opportunity cost. The opportunity cost of labor is not zero. It is a false notion that local government projects create benefits equal to additional employment times the wage rate. Wages are a cost incurred in producing services that yield benefits. We assume that each worker has a positive opportunity cost (i.e., there is something else individuals could be doing with their time), and that leisure is preferred to work. Given involuntary unemployment, it is reasonable to assume that some percentage of increased earnings would not have been earned in the absence of a particular project. However, only a portion of any increase in earned income should be considered as benefits permitting either higher personal consumption or increased tax revenue.

Volunteers

In the United States large numbers volunteer in public safety, the arts, health services, and in providing food and shelter to the homeless. About 28% of these volunteers work in government agencies. Volunteer hours can be summed and divided by total hours in an average work week to determine the number of full-time equivalent volunteers.

What value should be used as a shadow wage for volunteer labor? If volunteer time is shadow priced at zero, then the cost benefit ratio is grossly exaggerated. On the other hand, the ratio may consistently be close to one or negative if volunteer time is valued at a prevailing wage rate. Sensitivity analysis using boundary values between zero and the actual potential wage rate of volunteers assists in identifying the contribution of volunteer labor.[3]

Is the contribution of volunteer labor a cost? Or is it a benefit? In most cases, the value created by volunteers is a cost. After all, these volunteers could have been "employed" elsewhere. There is an opportunity cost in redirecting volunteers' efforts to the proposed project.

If the costs of recruiting, training, and monitoring volunteers are not elsewhere accounted for in terms of this particular project, these costs must be added onto the shadow cost of volunteer services.

The Nonlinearity of Costs and Benefits

Realistically, neither average costs nor average benefits are likely to remain constant. In both the short and long run, average and marginal costs tend to increase as firm output increases. It may be quite reasonable to assume that building maintenance cost per student remains constant on adding 20 more students to present facilities, but adding 60 additional students generally increases average cost. Also, the per person or marginal cost of reducing the first 20% of contaminants flowing into the river is likely less than reducing the next 20% (an example of average costs increasing with output). In the short run with fixed costs, production costs per unit (i.e., average costs) increase at some point as output expands. In the long run, internal and external diseconomies increase both average and marginal costs.

On the other hand, benefits tend to decline with additional units of consumption or when usage approaches capacity. The 50th versus 10th park outing per year yields fewer benefits and per person benefits for a lightly used highway are higher than per person benefits for crowded and congestion roads.

Consider three distinct cases:

1. Costs are constant over a range of output but increased consumption is subject to decreasing marginal benefits. If the proposed project were to lower (increase) user costs, consumer surplus would increase (decrease), and optimal consumption increase (decrease).
2. Benefits are constant but marginal costs increase due to diminishing returns. If the proposed project were to increase (decrease) production costs, consumption, and optimal output would decrease (increase).
3. Both costs and benefits are linear and, thus, a point of optimal output does not exist. In this instance, cost effective analysis (CEA), given a finite amount residents are willing to pay, may actually be preferred to CBA.

CBA deals with these technicalities by making the simplifying assumption that costs, benefits, or both are relatively linear for the range of output under consideration. The extent to which rudimentary CBA can legitimately ignore nonlinearity depends on the size of the distortion.

Summary of What You Have Learned in Chapter 6

Upon conclusion of this chapter, you should be able to:

- explain how CBA acts as a tool to limit official discretion;
- outline the positive and negative effects of user fees;
- realize that wages are costs, although a portion of these costs represent benefits to the previously unemployed;
- assess the value of volunteer labor;
- eliminate dubious benefits and make realistic assumption concerning macro stabilization, economic growth, and income distribution.
- recognize the potential for the assumption of linear costs and benefits to create distortions;

Introducing Cost Benefit Analysis to the Nonspecialist

When those difficult cases occur, they are difficult, chiefly because while we have them under consideration, all the reasons pro and con are not present to the mind at the same time; but sometimes one set present themselves, and at other times another, the first being out of sight. Hence the various purposes or inclinations that alternately prevail, and the uncertainty that perplexes us. To get over this, my way is to divide half a sheet of paper by a line into two columns; writing over the one Pro, and over the other Con.

—Benjamin Franklin (1772)

Chapter 7 Preview

When you have completed reading this chapter you will:

- be directed to existing cost benefit analysis (CBA) reference sources;
- realize the value of replicating or modifying existing CBA studies;
- evaluate alternative methods for quantifying recreational benefits;
- consider the process, using a nutritional program as an example, through which educational programs translate into benefits;
- begin to understand, in terms of a public library, how CBA analysts proceed to establish benefit standing in terms of users and residents.

Cost Benefit Analysis and the Nonspecialist

Is it reasonable to expect bureaucrats, local officials, and residents to comprehend and conduct CBA? CBA as presented in scholarly economic journals, in federal government handbooks, and in reports generated by professional consultants appears to require technical skills beyond the expertise of most local decision makers. Hence, politics and private interests inevitably trump deliberative decision making in the absence of some rational means to assess public proposals. Rather than rubber stamping proposals advocated by government employees and "experts," those charged with making local government decisions can learn to understand and effectively use CBA.

What basic competencies does CBA require? Excluding those proudly proclaiming their phobia to math or economic scarcity, CBA, as a technique, is generally accessible to those willing to apply it. Discounting future flows and calculating future and present values are curriculum standards in most States for senior high school finite math (e.g., Tennessee Mathematics Standards). All introductory economics textbooks include sections on opportunity, marginal, and variable costs. Almost all these books refer to productive and allocative efficiency, public and private goods, as well as consumer and producer surplus.

In getting started with CBA, decision makers have access to step-by-step handbooks as well as existing studies explicitly detailing their assumptions and methods.

Available CBA Resources

CBA manuals are available on the Web. A good source to begin with is the Australian *Handbook of Cost-Benefit Analysis* (2006). Follow that with *Circular A-4: Regulatory Analysis* of the U.S. Office of Management and Budget (2003). The European Commission's *Guide to Cost-Benefit Analysis* emphasizes feasibility and risk for large multiple state projects, and is less useful for rudimentary assessment of local projects. Those determined to master CBA can turn to a 500+ page Canadian document, *Transportation Cost and Benefit Analysis* (2009).

All recommended sources use spreadsheets, graphs, and algebra for dealing with risk, discounting, and consumer or producer surplus. Several handbooks, written on an advanced scholarly level, state that no prior knowledge of economics is required. It is probably hubristic to suggest that no training in economics or accounting is required.

After wading through "time preferences for nonmonetized benefits and costs," "dead weight loss," and "asymmetric information" (terms commonly found in these documents), it is understandable that officials would allocate large portions of their budgets to contracting out CBA rather than tackle it internally. Two questions remain: Are these reports actually being read by those who commission them? Are they understood by those commissioning them? Do decision makers shop for a consultant consistent with his or her bias?

Fortunately, work in academia, consultancies, and government is making CBA more easily accessible. CBA "apps" are unavailable at present but very much needed, given their potential of offering officials an affordable and effective assessment tool.[1] Meanwhile, they must rely on a few simple guidelines. In the future, these guidelines may evolve into standards increasing the public's confidence in CBA for projects associated with social, health, and educational goals.[2]

Uncovering Ways to Proceed from Existing CBA Reports

The best means to become somewhat proficient in CBA is to study existing reports in order to learn techniques and methods for valuating costs and benefits. Here, we will briefly review how three local programs in recreation, nutrition, and library services surmount problems associated with determining costs and benefits.

Placing Values on Recreational Activities

In 1962, Federal agencies devised some methods for measuring separate values for publicly provided outdoor recreation. The first method arbitrarily values all visits to water related recreational facilities at $0.50, $1, or $1.60 per day. These are essentially value judgments and do not measure differences in site quality. The second method is to develop demand schedules based on cost of travel to the recreational area. Basing benefits received on travel costs again ignores recreational quality differences. The third method is to value public recreation in terms of using the resource in some other way. A problem with this last method is that the Grand Canyon, for example, presently has no clearly defined alternative use, whereas a modest bird-watching reserve has a high opportunity cost in agriculture. A fourth method conducts surveys to assess people's willingness to make trade-offs on distance and value between public and private attractions. Would you rather hike the dunes or visit the casino? The final method, adapted from the profit-seeking sectors, uses market simulations or controlled laboratory experiments to assess people's preferences. For example, respondents could be given a stipend to allocate between different recreational activities.[3]

Calculation of Benefits for a State Nutritional Program

CBA was used to evaluate a food and nutrition class that the state of Virginia offers homemakers with incomes at or below 150% of the poverty level.

Expected benefits are first calculated in terms of reduced health expenditures resulting from changes in behavior associated with nutrition-related health conditions. Earnings that would have been forgone due to lost workdays or death were subsequently used to represent benefits. The formula used to monetize benefits in term of reduced health expenditures is:

$$\text{Benefit} = A * B * C * D * E$$

where,

A = annual number of program graduates

B = incidence of disease or health condition in low-income population

C = incidence of disease or health condition related to nutrition

D = percent of graduates practicing nutritional behaviors identified by disease or health condition

E = present values for benefits associated with each nutrition-related health conditions

A sample calculation of benefits for one nutrition-related health condition (present value of benefits per person = $3000):

A = 3,100 annual graduates of the program

B = (0.10 * 3,100) = 310 graduates affected with one of the targeted health conditions

C = (0.25 * 310) = 77 number of graduates with the condition that could control their problem with better nutrition

D = (0.05 * 77) = 4 graduates expected to practice good nutrition

E = ($3,000 * 4) = $12,000 total present value of benefits for the 4 graduates with this particular manageable condition that could be expected to practice good nutrition

After benefits were summarized for each targeted disease or health condition and compared with total program costs, net benefits were positive. Net benefits remained positive even when researchers applied more restrictive benefit assumptions, such as a decrease over time of graduates persevering with good diets or when benefits in general were discounted at a higher rate.[4]

Cost Benefit Analysis to Justify the Value of Library Services

In 2002, the City of Skokie, Illinois relied on CBA to estimate the net dollar value of services provided by its public libraries. Those with standing in the decision are defined separately as patrons directly benefiting from lending services financed with annual operating revenue and residents in general who pay to build and capitalize libraries. Table 7.1 identifies library services provided and their respective users.

Table 7.1 Service-user matrix for Skokie, Illinois public libraries

Taxonomy	Households	Teachers	Businesses
Books	×	×	×
Repair manuals	×		
Staff help	×	×	×
Financial			×
Computer	×	×	×

The library study used two approaches to determine the value of library services. Hypothetical contingent valuation was used to survey residents with questions, such as:

Suppose that public libraries did not exist.
How much would your household be willing to pay per year to establish your public library as it exists today?

In addition, a hedonic index, based on the actual market value of books purchased by residents, is used to develop a shadow price for library services. Admittedly, these amounts are self-reported, not observed. Figure 7.1 shows a resident's demand for borrowing books on the left and for purchasing books on the right. The loss in producer surplus to bookstore's competing with public libraries for readership is ignored; hence, the supply curve per item (S) is linear.

Note that borrowing or transactional prices to users are positive due to late penalties and transportation costs. The shaded area in the diagram on the left is consumer surplus from borrowing books, media, and so forth. The value of this benefit is approximated by how many additional books, media, and so forth the user would purchase in the absence of a library. The CBA estimated positive benefits for library services exceeding all annual operating costs as well as capital costs, including land, buildings, furnishings, collections, computers, and vehicles. The process

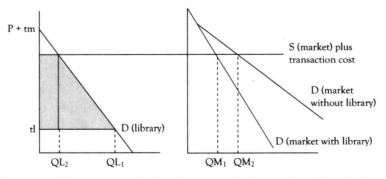

Figure 7.1 *Market price for books versus shadow price of borrowing for calculating consumer surplus benefit from library services*

Source: Elliott (2007).

Note: The left graph is a library user's demand for library books and the right diagram is demand for book purchases.

also determined that library users were much more likely to have higher incomes and advanced degrees than library nonusers.[5]

Bundled Proposals

CBA is incapable of handling continuous choice or project alternatives for sets of compatible alternatives. For example, two mutually exclusive projects such as Proposal A for new prisoner uniforms and Proposal B for prisoner uniform repair cannot be CBA assessed and ranked. However, if proposals are bundled together, the CBA criterion of positive net benefits may be applied to the whole package.

Bundling services into one CBA may be warranted. For example, consider Indiana's expansion of student testing. Presently, formal testing includes End of Course Assessments, Course-Aligned Assessments, the National Assessment of Educational Progress, and Assessment of Readiness for College and Careers. The State annually spends more than a billion dollars alone on the Indiana State Test of Educational Progress (ISTEP); indirect costs for teachers, counselors, para-professionals, and principals associated with administrating this and other tests are not included. Meanwhile, there have been few attempts to quantify test validity for educational quality or improvement in student learning per dollar spent.

Standardized testing, in general, is worthwhile. However, individual standardized assessments are not mutually exclusive in terms of benefits. CBA could bundle the full costs of all tests to accurately quantify benefits received. Then, through a process of elimination, certain tests could be deemed redundant and abandoned.

Rent Seeking

Conflict is inevitable when programs result in involuntary transfers between individuals. Individuals will invest resources to increase transfers to themselves. This behavior is called "rent seeking." There is considerable efficiency loss in collective decisions due to rent seeking behavior. CBA, alone, cannot fully compensate for this, but listing all costs and benefits could reduce rent seeking behavior. Ignoring distributional conflicts is in the long run costlier than dealing directly with conflicts of interest.

With CBA, assumptions, costs, and benefits are explicitly stated to mini-mize the efficiency loss endemic to collective decision making. CBA, as a means of evaluating proposals, is not a "free lunch," but cost per proposal is reduced as local officials gain proficiency.

Summary of What You Have Learned in Chapter 7

Upon conclusion of this chapter, you should be able to:

- reference the Australian *Handbook of Cost-Benefit Analysis* (2006) followed with *Circular A-4: Regulatory Analysis* of the U.S. Office of Management and Budget (2003);
- replicate and modify existing CBA studies to assess local government proposals;
- apply monetary values for benefits received through local government programs in recreational, educational, and lending library services;
- set up matrices of services offered and their users;
- differentiate between users and general public, as well as between operating and capital costs;
- show why alternate proposals for a range of continuous services are not mutually exclusive and therefore inappropriate for CBA analysis.

CHAPTER 8

Cost Benefit Analysis of Proposed New Regulations

There is only one difference between a bad economist and a good one: the bad economist confines himself to the visible effect; the good economist takes into account both the effect that can be seen and those effects that must be foreseen.

—Frederic Bastiat (1801–1850)

Chapter 8 Preview

When you have completed reading this chapter you will:

- be aware of "regulatory capture" and the use and misuse of cost benefit analysis (CBA) in local government regulation;
- consider how the compliance costs of regulation affect price and output;
- differentiate between regulations affecting parties directly involved with a transaction and those associated with third party external effects;
- assess regulatory effectiveness by referring to five questions;
- know how one city used CBA to develop regulations for taxi services, business or occupational licenses, and building/construction permits.

Many municipalities have regulations requiring businesses and home owners to clear sidewalks within 24 hours after a snowfall and to mow their lawns such that grass does not exceed 10 inches in height. In addition, municipalities may rule that no more than two individuals unrelated by law or birth occupy single-unit residences. Shops may not open until 12 noon on Sundays.

In previous chapters, we focused on CBA's relevance for explicit government programs using taxes and subsidies to nudge production toward an optimal level. In this chapter, we study CBA with respect to local government regulations mandating private and government behavior; these regulations or mandates generally require that a firm or household do something. Total implementation costs of new regulations should necessarily be less than increased benefits. In addition to private compliance costs, new regulations increase government enforcement costs and often require intra-government reports. For example, a new regulation on local property increases owner costs in terms of time and money, and government revenue must be directed toward inspection, reporting, and perhaps ensuring that vacant and abandoned properties are brought up to code. Regulations increase costs. The benefits of increased regulation are to reduce harmful social behaviors.

Regulatory Effects on Price and Output

Regulations result in intended and unintended costs. CBA makes a good faith effort to identify and quantify all compliance and enforcement costs. Compliance costs are borne by all sectors: households, firms, and government. The government, of course, assumes the costs of enforcing compliance for all new and existing regulations.

It is often incorrectly assumed that increased costs to firms in complying with new regulations are either internalized in the form of reduced profits or simply passed on to consumers in higher prices. The actual effect (the cost of regulation) is usually some combination of reduced profits, higher prices charged consumers, decreased production and consumption, and the exit of some firms from the market.

A review of Figure 4.2 demonstrates price and quantity effects of any regulation designed to correct for unregulated negative market outcomes. Industry regulations increase private firms' cost in supplying goods and services. Increasing production costs shifts the industry' supply curve to the left, raising equilibrium price and reducing equilibrium quantity. Consider the case in which private individuals are subjected to increased occupational and licensing requirements. If their clients internalize these costs by paying higher prices, demand decreases reducing equilibrium quantity. The CBA analyst must therefore realize that regardless of the sector internalizing costs, **the burden is shifted and shared** between both producer and consumer. Note, that in regulated industries, quantity produced declines. Firms, unable to compete with additional costs, leave the market. Households, unwilling to pay a higher price, reallocate their incomes.

Consider how CBA costs are affected by increased training and licensing requirements for barbers. Assume that the actual cost per haircut increase to barbers for recertification training, forfeited earnings, and licensing fees is about $1.50 per haircut. Let the increase in licensing fees collected more or less equals the increase in government enforcement costs. Depending on client responsiveness to price, it may be that barbers can shift two-thirds of the increase in their costs to clients, resulting in a price increase of $1 per haircut (2/3 * $1.50). Two methods of estimating CBA costs if the new regulation were to be approved are:

1. The number of haircuts (x) multiplied by $1.50.
2. The number of haircuts multiplied by market increase in price (x * $1) plus the increased costs to barbers (x * $.50).

Realize that one or the other of the two methods listed can be applied because each method alone approximates the opportunity cost of reallocated resources. It should be noted, however, both methods fail to account for the deadweight loss of any income forfeited by barbers exiting the profession or benefits forfeited by the lowered frequency of client haircuts purchased. A more detailed estimate would (correctly) take into account the likely decrease in the number of haircuts due to the increased cost of providing and the increased price of purchasing the service.

Consider, now, the benefits of such a regulation. CBA benefits consist of an estimation of the dollar value of injuries prevented by regulating higher standards for barber certification. Barbers could possibly earn higher total income due to higher entry barriers; indeed some would argue that barbers are most likely advocates for such a measure Higher income for barbers, however, is not a targeted benefit. Any increase in barbers' income is represented as a cost to clients paying a higher price per haircut. The goal of CBA is to represent the intensity of consumer preferences for safety and the effectiveness of regulation in reducing injuries and negative externalities.

New regulations require that public sector agencies be created or refocused, employees hired, and reports filed. In addition, efforts in policing a regulation inevitably contributes to increasing public sector costs. In applying regulatory CBA, proposed benefits must be compared with all increases in private and public compliance and enforcement costs.

CBA as the Wrong Tool for Justifying Government Action to Advance Net Private Gain

Interest groups, private industry, and government bureaucracies are empowered by the inexperience of decision-making officials. The results are regulations benefiting private interests at the expense of the general public. Officials can be captured by those they seek to regulate, because the regulated are often better informed than those regulating. On the other hand, officials themselves are tempted to use regulations for their own personal political advantage.

Regulations contrary to the public interest include price supports, restrictions on market entry, subsidies, tax abatements, suppression of alternate technologies, and so on. Such measures concentrate benefits toward a small number of favored beneficiaries while disbursing small per unit costs to the general public.

Due to relatively low coordinating costs, interest groups with much to gain are more likely to co-op local government. Regulatory proposals restricting liberty at public expense, regardless of the size of benefits to a sub-set of private interests, should be summarily dismissed.

CBA as the Wrong Tool for Justifying Exceptions from the Rule of Law

Note carefully that we are not suggesting that measures to enforce the Constitution, Bill of Rights, or general rule of law be subject to CBA. Unfortunately, the term "cost benefit" is often used indiscriminately to advance proposals contrary to law and constitutional rights.

For example, it may be the case that a heritage tree stands in the way and obstructs $3 million in potential development. A law prohibiting the removal of designated legacy trees is a legal issue, and any exception should not be determined using CBA methodology. Existing property rights are in conflict with the value of alternative uses for the land on which the tree is standing. Perhaps, the $3 million figure in potential opportunity cost is a valuable piece of information to those charged with making exceptions or ruling on public domain. However, using "cost benefit" to estimate the value of potential private (gain) opportunities is quite different from CBA as presented in this text. CBA is presented here as a tool, estimating benefits and costs based on actual market or market-like transactions with respect to a specific proposal over which officials have discretion. CBA is appropriately performed or commissioned by officials, with no dog-in-the-race, ruling in trust for the general public on policy *versus* legal matters.

CBA that addresses income distribution and justice is called regulatory impact analysis (RIA). Consistent with other chapters in this book, our discussion on local government regulation focuses neither on income distribution nor fairness considerations.

Local Ordinances

The focus in this chapter is on local government regulations or ordinances associated with private transactions in production and consumption that may result in personal injury or be associated with a social externality.

An ordinance is a statute or regulation generally enacted by local government. These regulations deal with consumer and worker safety, driver and automobile licensing, building safety, noise abatement, live poultry within city limits, trash removal, and property maintenance. Benefits consist of restricting behavior that is legal but nevertheless could result in harm to the well-being of at least one person engaged in a transaction or to society in general. Costs include compliance expenditures borne by government agencies, private firms, and households and, to a lesser extent, enforcement costs borne by government.

Some regulations deal with transactions between residents without significantly affecting third parties; others deal with transactions that predominately affect the community in general. In the case of restaurant sanitary practices, the transaction is between owner and customer (the customer is the potential victim). In banning loud noises after 10:00 pm, there is no direct transaction between the one inflicting injury and his or her victim but rather third party social costs. CBA applies to both types of ordinances.[1]

A Regulatory Proposal with Limited External Costs or Benefits

In the absence of regulations dealing with employee safety, firms attract labor to dangerous positions by paying higher than average wages for similarly skilled workers. Similarly, lower rents are charged on buildings that are subject to noise or otherwise appear unsafe to potential renters. Workers and renters internalize these risks. However, individuals may be ill-informed concerning their long-term interests. If workers, renters, or consumers were fully informed with respect to risk and had alternative options, the market could work in reducing harmful outcomes or in compensating those accepting risk.

CBA discerns responsible regulations by calculating the benefits of moving to a more optimal level of resident well-being and to measure the cost of doing so. Government can in certain instances over-regulate when actual and synthetic markets have independently achieved an optimal level of safety. Compliance and enforcement costs for accident prevention beyond this level result in net loss.

Insufficient information and unequal bargaining power justify government regulation. CBA assists in identifying whether or not a proposed regulation targets the desired objective. Comparing costs and benefits of two different regulatory methods increases the likelihood of reaching the objective. For example, should regulations act a priori to prevent accidents from ever occurring or should regulations compensate those harmed by requiring firms to bear higher costs in the form of fines, taxes, or social insurance? The choice depends on known technology of how best to avoid accidents. CBA is a means of making clear to both decision makers and the general public that regulatory compliance and enforcement costs exist (note carefully that regulatory and compliance costs are indeed real and sometimes substantial). In most cases, a substantial portion of these costs will be shifted onto consumers in the form of higher prices, lowered output, and exit from the industry of firms and jobs that cannot meet the new regulatory standards.

A Regulatory Proposal with Significant External Costs or Benefits

Consider a case in which external costs to the general public exist but have to a large extent been internalized. In Napa, CA, residents transact with the city to purchase water for their lawns. However, the California State Water Resources Control Board is considering new regulations. One proposal requires towns to further limit storm-water discharge into the Napa River and the other proposal requires cities to monitor run-offs of lawn water into storm sewers. If adopted, the first measure could raise the city of Napa's annual storm-water discharge costs from about $400,000 to about $3.3 million in the first year of operation. With regard to the second proposal, local government would have to locate owners of lawn sprinklers running too long, turn off their water, and issue citations. At issue is the relationship between the proposed regulations and their targeted objective, improved water quality.

Napa officials suspect that the Board's new regulations are aimed at controlling real estate development rather than water quality considerations. Officials feel that they have already made progress in improving water quality and incremental measures would be quite costly. Because the city currently educates residents about overwatering and charges a premium for heavy water use, the problem of incidental runoff contaminants has been internalized. Exorbitant increased costs for households and firms would yield less benefits than targeting the real spillover issues outside local control. At present, the city of Napa can enforce these regulations on firms and households but schools and other government buildings are exempted. Local regulations also do not apply to property outside their jurisdiction that discharges into the Napa River.

Most residents are in favor of using regulation to reduce negative externalities in environmental pollution, crime, and road accidents. There is a demand for the reduction of outcomes perceived as undesirable. We benefit most from trying to prevent the most likely and harmful behaviors. Each prevention entails cost in the form of time, personal liberty, compliance, and enforcement. Should government try to reduce all these negatives to zero? No. At some point, the cost of prevention exceeds expected benefit.

For example, given an increasing marginal cost of noise prevention and a decreasing marginal benefit of prevention, a degree of noise, at least during certain times of the day, will be tolerated by the relevant locality. Regulations that attempt to curtail noise, lawn water runoffs, or other negative externalities beyond optimal reductions are inefficient in terms of opportunity costs.

Applying CBA to Existing Regulations

In 1991, Indianapolis Mayor Stephen Goldsmith established the Regulatory Study Commission (RSC) and charged it with weeding out bad regulations and conducting CBA on all new ones. The RSC posed five questions, helpful to analysts using CBA to assess newly proposed regulations:

1. How would the regulation benefit the consumer or public?
2. How would the regulation benefit the regulated parties?
3. How would the regulation increase costs to residents in general?
4. How would the regulation affect costs of the regulated parties?
5. What administrative or enforcement costs would be paid by taxpayers?

It is helpful to consider how the Indianapolis study approached the costs and benefits of local regulations.

To study the effect of then highly regulated taxi services in Indianapolis, the RSC compared empirical studies of prices and services in other cities. The results, given Uber, Lift, and other platforms, now appear to us to be obvious and obsolete. The number of illegal taxis, was higher in strongly regulated markets, and this number was identified as a good measure of the extent to which current legal transportation services failed to meet expected demand. Actual taxi service complaints in Indianapolis were, therefore, recorded and logged by the city controller's office. Associated low *versus* high taxicab prices in competitive markets were adjusted for vehicle quality, wheelchair lifts, and service availability to lower income, elderly, and disabled clients. It was determined that allowing unregulated "flag-drop" charges, stated upfront to all passengers, increased the availability of less remunerative short-run pickups. Permission to charge lower fares combined with "maximum fare ceilings" worked to prevent gouging of one time out-of-town visitors.

States, in general, regulate occupations by licensing doctors, lawyers, hairdressers, electricians, and so on. Regulation of occupations is justified as a means of protecting public health and safety only if government is better able than the general public to determine quality. To deregulate, the RSC in Indianapolis freed certain local businesses or occupations from the expense of annual licensing in return for a required one time no-fee registration. By studying enforcement and application histories, the RSC determined which industries to exempt. Those selected had seen little or no enforcement activity in the previous decade. Not a single enforcement action had ever been taken against unlicensed used car dealers, whose compliance rate for proper city licensing was less than 20 percent. Assuming that it takes 45 minutes of employee time to relicense, the benefits to all dealers from deregulation were appraised in terms of not having to pay fees and the value of work time lost in recertification:

B_f = Total dollar of fees collected in the previous year + 0.75
($31.80 hourly employee compensation, indirect personnel expenses, and overhead).[2]

It is hard to imagine a situation in which individual home owners are prohibited from tackling low-risk Do-It-Yourself projects without government permission. Yet, little by little, Indianapolis ordinances increased permits required of property owners prior to initiating projects. Approval, in some instances, involved four separate agencies. The first task assumed by the Commission in evaluating regulatory effectiveness was to estimate the extent to which property owners were in compliance with existing rules requiring a permit to replace windows:

1. Potential Annual Window Replacements = (Estimated Windows per House * Number of Homes)/Average Life of a Window

2. Permit Compliance Rate = Annual Window Replacement Permit Requests/Potential Window Replacements.[3]

The RSC estimated that less than 1 percent of home owners were in compliance with the window replacement permit regulation. A proposal sought to reengineer the local building permit process while strengthening customer protection. Permits for certain low-impact repairs were eliminated, a single building permit was substituted for various subcontractor permits, and specified city employees where assigned responsibility for certain types of permits. Penalties for shoddy work and violating agreements increased, and enforcement mechanisms were toughened.[4]

Due to problems of scale across firms and communities, the advantages of using CBA on a national level may be limited to serving as a veto mechanism in assessing newly proposed regulations.[5] For all levels of government, CBA does play a valid role in identifying costly obsolete regulations that no longer serve their purpose. On a local level, CBA offers substantial value in small-scale regulatory reform.

Summary of What You Have Learned in Chapter 8

Upon conclusion of this chapter, you should be able to:

- differentiate between regulations that needlessly result in providers exiting markets from those that internalize costs to firms and consumers in order to target a desired public objective;
- explain how regulations increase the price of consumption, decrease profits, and restrict the quantity of goods and services exchanged;
- use CBA to identify and quantify the extent to whether a proposed regulation targets the desired objective;
- to identify and quantify the costs of compliance and enforcement of a proposed regulation;
- compare markets in like cities to determine the role of regulations in providing or obstructing the provision of services demanded;
- analyze techniques for measuring regulatory compliance.

CHAPTER 9

Case Study: Contracting Versus a Municipal Animal Control Shelter

We like to imagine coherent government planning. We like to think policy actions are predicated on careful and intelligent anticipation of consequences. But the nature of the beast is otherwise. Any rational coordination of means and ends goes out the window as soon as the political scramble for subsidies begins.

—Holman W. Jenkins, Jr.

Case studies, templates, proto-types, and standards are needed to refine and make cost benefit analysis (CBA) accessible to local decision makers. In this chapter, a CBA case study compares a proposal to accept a 3-year contract with the Humane Society *versus* an expansion of the present city owned and operated animal control program. Counties and town official are often confronted with similar decisions such as government-operated waste and leaf removal *versus* contracting out for these services.

Calculations in this study on animal control are spreadsheet based, using standard net present value (NPV) and present value (PV) formulas built into the software. Cases in this and the following chapters represent CBA proto-types.

CBA reports are generally divided into four sections. The "**Introduction**" summarizes the default position and the proposal being considered. The "**Methodology**" section defines terms and data specific to the project and presents the decision criteria. The "**Analysis**" section outlines costs and benefits and solves for net benefits. If discount rate or other types of sensitivity analysis are provided, any unambiguous results are explained. The "**Conclusion**" consists of a fairly firm recommendation and possibly the analyst's evaluation of contingencies affecting results. Suggestions for further study are sometimes included in CBA reports.

Introduction

A local resident, who has managed a private business for over three decades, recommenced to Hometown's Town Council a proposal for their consideration. In particular, as a pet owner, the resident was concerned about Hometown's plan to build an expensive new animal control facility. The Town Council created a committee charged with determining if the proposal had merit. The following analysis is loosely based on an actual study in providing animal control services.[1]

This particular CBA compares two options: expanding Hometown's current animal control operation or accepting a 3-year contract offered by the Humane Society for similar services. Three possible borrowing rates test for discount rate sensitivity. For those uncomfortable with PV calculations, a graph of undiscounted costs and benefits for each year offers an intuitive understanding. A shadow price representing the per capita value of animal control services is developed; this shadow price is based on the present willingness to pay for animal control services by residents of an adjoining town that we will call Downton. The figure for Hometown was adjusted upward because Hometown has a lower population density relative to land mass than Downton. In dealing with pets, raccoons, and other wildlife, Hometown has higher expected costs per person for animal control services.

Net benefits here do not reflect before and after consumer surplus derived from two points on a demand curve. The implicit assumption is rather that the choice has been made to offer the same level of service as that provided in an adjoining town. The analysis compares two alternative ways of delivering this same level of service. CBA calculations are presented in Table 9.1.

The Methodology

A shadow price is needed to represent total annual animal control benefits received. The total annual value of Hometown animal control services is

Table 9.1 Cost benefit case study assessing two options: 1. 3-year proposed city contract with the Humane Society 2. Expanded municipal animal control service

Option 1: Hometown contracts with the Humane Society	Humane Society Contract Option					
	Year 1	Year 2	Year 3	PV 3%	PV 5%	PV 7%
Present Value of Costs:						
Humane Society Contract Proposed to City	170,000	170,000	170,000	($480,863.93)	($462,952.16)	($446,133.73)
City Pays for Five Full Time Employees	150,000	150,000	150,000	($424,291.70)	($408,487.20)	($393,647.41)
Five Vans Maintained by City	70,000	70,000	70,000	($198,002.79)	($190,627.36)	($183,702.12)
Construction of Additional Runs	200,000	–	–	($194,174.76)	($190,476.19)	($186,915.89)
Space for Additional 250 Cats	50,000	–	–	($48,543.69)	($47,619.05)	($46,728.97)
Donated Services	50,000	50,000	50,000	($141,430.57)	($136,162.40)	($131,215.80)
Total Costs	690,000	440,000	440,000	-$1,487,307.44	-$1,436,324.37	-$1,388,343.92
Present Value of Benefits:						
Animal Owner Fees- 25% of annual operating budget	97,500	97,500	97,500	$275,789.61	$265,516.68	$255,870.81
Private Cash Donations	30,000	30,000	30,000	$84,858.34	$81,697.44	$78,729.48
Donated Space for Cats (Bank)	50,000	–	–	$48,543.69	$47,619.05	$46,728.97
Net Value/Alternate Use of Existing SB Facility	100,000	–	–	$97,087.38	$95,238.10	$93,457.94
Animal Control Benefits (see Notes)	343,971	343,971	343,971	$972,960.28	$936,718.35	$902,688.61
Total Benefits	621,471	471,471	471,471	$1,479,239.29	$1,426,789.61	$1,377,475.83
Net Benefits				($8,068.15)	($9,534.76)	($10,868.09)
Net Qualitative Benefits:						
Present Euthanasia Rate	50%					

Option 2: Hometown expands existing municipal animal control services						
				South Bend New Facility Option		
	Year 1	Year 2	Year 3	PV 3%	PV 5%	PV 7%
Present Value of Costs:						
Feasibility and Contracting Costs of Bldg.	120,000	—	—	($116,504.85)	($114,285.71)	($112,149.53)
Principle plus Interest on Debt	58,334	116,667	116,667	($273,371.62)	($262,157.94)	($251,654.26)
Maintenance on Bldg.	30,000	60,000	60,000	($140,590.47)	($134,823.45)	($129,421.58)
Nine Full Time Employees	400,000	400,000	400,000	-$1,131,444.54	-$1,089,299.21	-$1,049,726.42
Maintaining Five Vans	70,000	70,000	70,000	($198,002.79)	($190,627.36)	($183,702.12)
Other Expenses	30,000	30,000	30,000	($84,858.34)	($81,697.44)	($78,729.48)
Total Costs	708,334	676,667	676,667	-$1,944,772.62	-$1,872,891.12	-$1,805,383.39
Present Value of Benefits:						
Animal Owner Fees- 14% annual operating budget	70,000	70,000	70,000	$198,002.79	$190,627.36	$183,702.12
Potential Net Value of Bldg. to City	—	—	250,000	$228,785.41	$215,959.40	$204,074.47
Net Value/Alternate Use of Existing Facility	100,000	—	—	$97,087.38	$95,238.10	$93,457.94
Animal Control Benefits (see Notes)	343,971	343,971	343,971	$972,960.28	$936,718.35	$902,688.61
Total Benefits	513,971	413,971	663,971	$1,496,835.86	$1,438,543.20	$1,383,923.15
Net Benefits				($447,936.76)	($434,347.92)	($421,460.24)

Net Qualitative Benefits:
Present Euthanasia Rate   65%

Notes: Based on report of Fred Ferlic, "Testing Consolidation of Animal Control Make Sense," *South Bend Tribune*, August 8, 2011.
All payments are made and benefits received at the end of each period.
Animal Control Benefits: This is a proxy or shadow price representing the amount each resident is willing to pay annually for standard services. The amount used here is $3.10 for each resident each year; population is held constant for period. The figure is derived from the total expenses per resident paid in the neighboring town of Mishawaka for basic animal control services ($2.98) adjusted upward for South Bend given its lower populations density per square mile (2838 for Mishawaka versus 2468 for South Bend).

estimated at $3.40 per resident multiplied by the number of residents, assumed to remain constant. This shadow price is derived from the annual per resident cost of $2.98 in Downton. The Hometown amount per resident was adjusted upward by $.42 based on its lower population density per square mile (2,838 for Downton *versus* 2,468 for Hometown).

The Analysis

With two options each offering the same level of services, the goal is one of minimizing net costs rather than maximizing net benefits. Note that net benefits are negative for both options, regardless of the discount rate chosen. The CBA report would recommend contracting rather than expansion as the best option for minimizing loss.

Figure 9.1 presents undiscounted costs and benefits for each of the 3 years for the two options; Part a refers to a proposed contract with the Humane Society and Part b to the default municipality-operated service. Part a shows that the contract option yields positive benefits in Years 2 and 3. Part b shows that for the expanded municipal shelter default option costs exceed benefits for all 3 years. Figure 9.1 provides a limited and potentially misleading visual perspective. The present value of net benefits, which discounts costs and benefits using three different rates as shown in Table 9.1, is the preferred method. Note that neither Option 1 nor Option 2 in Table 9.1 has positive present values net benefits.

The time horizon for this case is based on a 3-year contract offered by the Humane Society. The option of expanding the present facility includes the value of ownership in year 3. Similarly, for infrastructure projects such as bridges and highways designed to last for 30 or more years, it is acceptable to use a shortened time horizon. In such cases, the PV of all future costs and benefits are included in the final year.

Conclusion

Any benefits, if the contract option is chosen, are contingent on private donations and the ability of the Humane Society to collect fees equal to 25% of its annual operating budget. An additional consideration is the effort and expense required for periodic contract renegotiation. Clearly,

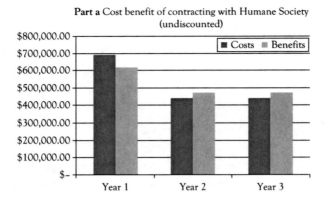

Part a Cost benefit of contracting with Humane Society (undiscounted)

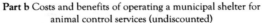

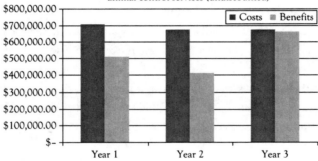

Part b Costs and benefits of operating a municipal shelter for animal control services (undiscounted)

Figure 9.1 Case study: Cost benefit comparison with Humane Society contract vs. expanded municipal shelter undiscounted costs and benefits

however, both options represent yearly expenditures exceeding the shadow price of $3.40 used to represent the value of such services per resident. The 3-year loss, discounting at 5%, is 9 cents for contracting versus $4.29 per resident for expansion.

Note: The actual City Council, on which this case is partially based, approved construction of a new expanded city-operated animal control shelter. It is too early to determine if actual budget data will confirm that residents' annual cost per person for animal control services greatly exceeds the $3.40 shadow price on which this hypothetical CBA case study is based. The cautionary lesson to be learned is that CBA analysis should be done prior to initiating a project and, ideally, revisited mid-project and beyond.

CHAPTER 10

Case Study: Cost Benefit Analysis for a Forty Acre Industrial Park Intended to Spawn Economic Development and Jobs

Nobody spends somebody else's money as carefully as he spends his own.
—Milton Friedman

Introduction

Suppose that the City's Redevelopment Commission's main business for this evening is to decide whether or not to convert a presently unused 40 acre parcel of land owned by the town into an industrial park. The default position is to reject the proposal and either hold the land or sell the undeveloped property. The chosen 10-year time horizon is based on how long it would take the City to pay the principal and interest on $1,000,000 in bonds to be issued for infrastructure and development costs. Interest and principal at a guaranteed annualized percentage borrowing rate of 2.7% would be paid at the end of each year. Job creation and economic development are the stated objectives of the project, but it should be noted that, from an economic efficiency point of view, total increased wages, including state and federal taxes, do not represent CBA benefits. Rather, the well-being of residents in the form of increased producer and consumer surplus represent true benefits. This case study highlights the importance of clearly identifying for whom the decision maker has fiduciary responsibility.

The CBA, presented in Table 10.1, is **not** an economic impact analysis estimating how changes in economic activity affect overall personal income. The purpose of CBA is simply to determine if net benefits to the relevant community as a whole are positive. The CBA analysis, as presented in Table 10.1, does not account for any off-setting effects resulting from the potential strategic response of nearby localities.

The Methodology

This case is based on one developed by the Local Government Center of the University of Wisconsin.[1] We realize that industrial parks may not fill as quickly as projected and guard against over optimism on wage income increases. We must again emphasize that no attempt is made to account for the likely response of surrounding communities.

Consider the calculation of benefits in terms of one newly employed worker's disposable income. An unemployed worker's opportunity cost in terms of leisure or home production (care of dependents, home maintenance, etc.) is positive. An estimate for benefits forfeited by entering into paid employment is subtracted from earned market wages. The difference represents benefits gained by the previously unemployed. In quantifying wage benefits, we should realize that some newly created positions will likely be filled either by those presently employed or by those commuting from outside the town.

In this case study, potential increases in wages (acres developed *jobs created per acre* annual income) are a source of benefits for the local economy ($6,630,000 in year 10). To approximate this potential increase in producer surplus (higher wage income for those offering their labor), the total potential wage amount is reduced first by 25% for federal and states taxes and then reduced by 50% to account for benefits to out-of-town employees, job transfers within town, and the opportunity costs of home production and leisure, forfeited by the previously unemployed.

CBA exercises sometimes include a section quantifying or at least indicating the direction of the extent to which one group transfers costs, benefits, or both to another. In this case study, resident taxpayers, including present owners of industrial property, finance and assume risk that may or may not benefit them personally. It is likely that the project will result in distributing net benefits to the unemployed and new business owners or tenants.

New infrastructure could, however, benefit residents in general. In CBA, transfers between subgroups can be treated as an accounting convention allocating costs and benefits but these transfers do not affect total net benefits. This is a critical distinction because the purpose of CBA is to determine if net benefits to all those, for whom the decision makers act in trust, are positive. We acknowledge transfers, hypothesize about their direction, but do not attempt to quantify them. The focus is on net benefits for residents as a whole within a specified time period.

Qualitative benefits to be derived for the proposal are listed in Table 10.1; these include improved aesthetics and community morale.

The Analysis

Using public borrowing or tax funds to develop industrial parks, implies:

1. At the end of the relevant period, total income net of federal and state taxes earned within the local community exceeds resident income prior to the project; this increase in income or property values is generally expected to result in tax revenue compensating taxpayers for initial costs. In addition, households experiencing a net increase in post-tax income are enabled to privately consume and save more than they would have in the absence of the project. Net benefit gains are due to two factors, more efficient use of the community's land resource and value created by labor currently less than optimally employed.

2. Such projects affect various sectors of the economy differently. Existing owners of commercial buildings may experience a decrease in rental income as the supply of rental property increases. If the expected increase in gross income is realized, certain sectors such as construction, real estate brokers, and the previously unemployed stand to gain from both the net loss of present owners earning lower rents and taxpayer subsidies.

3. There is a probability that benefits will not be realized. In this case study, the CPA shows that all newly developed acreage is sold and

Table 10.1 *Case study: Cost-benefit analysis for proposed industrial park developed by city to improve local economy or employment 40 acres, 10-year time horizon, and 2.7% Discount rate*

	Year 1	Year 2	Year 3	Year 4	Year 5	Year 6	Year 7	Year 8	Year 9	Year 10	PV 2.7%	Resident Impact
Present Value of Costs:												
a. land	(100,000)										$ (97,370.98)	Negative
b. Infrastructure	(123,820)	(123,820)	(123,820)	(123,820)	(123,820)	(123,820)	(123,820)	(123,820)	(123,820)	(113,820)	$ (1,072,66.35)	Negative
c. Plant Construction	(30,954)	(30,954)	(30,954)	(30,954)	(30,954)	(30,954)	(30,954)	(30,954)	(30,954)	(30,954)	$ (268,132.93)	Negative
d. Administration	(250,000)	(250,000)	(250,000)	(250,000)	(250,000)	(250,000)	(250,000)	(250,000)	(250,000)	(250,000)	$ (2,165,575.74)	Negative
e. Fire, Police, Insurance	(50,000)	(50,000)	(50,000)	(50,000)	(50,000)	(50,000)	(50,000)	(50,000)	(50,000)	(50,000)	$ (433,115.15)	Negative
											$ (4,036,761.16)	
Present Value of Benefits:												
h. Property Tax Revenue			114,500	229,000	343,500	458,000	458,000	458,000	458,000	458,000	$ 2,463,955.81	Positive
i. Local Income Tax Revenue	—	—	13,250	26,500	39,750	53,000	53,000	53,000	53,000	53,000	$ 285,130.26	Positive
j. Disposable Income	—	—	496,900	993,800	1,490,700	1,987,600	1,987,600	1,987,600	1,987,600	1,987,600	$ 10,692,922.65	Transfers
k. Reduced Social Service Costs	—	—	50,000	100,000	150,000	200,000	200,000	200,000	200,000	200,000	$ 1,075,963.24	Positive
l. Sale of Improved Property	—	—	500,000	500,000	500,000	500,000					$ 1,774,825.43	
											$ 14,517,971.96	
Net Benefits											$ 10,481,210.80	

Net Qualitative Benefits:
Aesthetics of Area
Community Morale
Identification with Locality

Notes:

All payments occur at the end of each period.

Cost a. Market value of the 40 acres presently owned by the city.

Cost b. Payments of principal and interest on bonds issued to build roads.

Cost c. Payments of principal and interest on bonds issued to develop lots.

Benefit h. The MIL rate is $11.45. As compared with before-project property values, total residential and business property values increase by $1,000,000 for each acre developed.: For Year 3, $10 million. Year 4, $20 million. Year 5, $30 million, Year 6, $40 million. Year 7, $40 million, Year 8, $40 million, Year 9, $40 million, Year 10, $40 million. Additional property taxes represent the benefit value of any new infrastructure.

Benefit i. Each acre generates 5 new jobs paying $26,500 on average. Increases in local income tax revenue equals 1% or $260 per job for residents and non-residents.

Benefit j. Wage income is adjusted downward by 25% to account for federal, state, and local taxes; note that local income taxes are included as Benefit I, but federal and states taxes are excluded. Each new job, therefore, increases disposable income by $19,875. Only one half of this amount ($9,938) used as a proxy for the increase in producer and consumer surplus per job; this reduction is a judgment call accounting for nonresidents taking positions and residents transferring between jobs as well as the opportunity cost of leisure/home production forfeited by those now employed.

Benefit k. For each reduction in unemployment by 5 in the resident and commuting population, social costs for welfare/crime reduced by $5000.

Benefit l. In each of Years 3, 4, and 5, five acres in the Industrial Park owned by the City are sold to private business. The project increased the value per acre by $100,000.

Although overall net benefits may be positive, certain individuals experience a net loss from this type of project. Costs are borne by residents and possibly existing landlords with benefits transferred to those receiving increased disposable income in profit and wages.

entered as benefits. This is likely only if the project is in line with a community's comparative advantage in the national or global supply chain.

4. Project advocates often represent private financial, political, or ideological interests in directing the economy away from or toward certain activities. Lobbyists can provide decision-makers with valuable information, but CBA ideally maintains its independence from and does not act on behalf of such interests.

In this case study, positive net benefits suggest that government, in the absence of a private developer, functions as prime mover to assist in using resources more efficiently. In analyzing the industrial park proposal, net benefits are positive because the existing opportunity costs for land and labor are lower than the value created by directing those same resources to alternative uses. If tax abatements are required to attract firms to the new industrial park or if a nearby town reacts strategically, any net benefits will be reduced.

Conclusion

Piling on dubious benefits for the unemployed, local retailers, renters of industrial property, construction interests, and real estate brokers must be avoided. Benefits consist of increased disposable income and perhaps infrastructure to be financed with increased tax revenue and the sale of improved property. Profits earned in the Industrial Park are likely distributed to out-of-town owners and financers, and no attempt has been made to include them in this case study.

In this case study, taxpayers guarantee interest and principal for 10 years and accept the risk that private buyers may not come forth to purchase the developed lots, that new jobs may not be created, and that local property and income taxes may not increase. The cost benefit analysis (CBA) process indeed raises questions about local government economic development activity. Do such projects have public good characteristics requiring government action? Could the undeveloped land be sold and be better managed by a private developer? Using tax funds for commercial activity may be irresponsible given the decision maker's fiduciary role; the taxpayer should be aware of the inevitable risk entailed in such activity. In fact, we may be dealing with uncertainty rather than risk. Indirect benefits are transferred risk free to those engaged in construction and real estate, for example; whereas, potential returns to the taxpayer have a distinct probability of being less than one.

The CBA for the Industrial Park proposal, presented in Table 10.1, suggests that the present undeveloped site and unemployed labor would be more efficiently utilized, if the project were approved. This assumes a low 2.7% borrowing rate for issuing 10-year bonds guaranteed by Hometown's taxpayers. Otherwise, the property continues unused or possibly sold to nontaxable entities, which legally are not required to contribute tax revenue for Hometown's infrastructure. Projected net benefits for this proposal, based on benefits to residents as a whole, are positive.

If you were a member of Hometown's Redevelopment Commission's would you be willing on the basis of information here to vote favorably on converting this presently unused parcel of land owned by the town into an industrial park?

CHAPTER 11

Case Study: Establishing a Recreational Program for the Disabled

What is a cynic? A man who knows the price of everything, and the value of nothing.

—Oscar Wilde

Introduction

Suppose that at the last Town Council meeting, parents, attending with children, advocated for a municipal recreational program serving disabled residents. At present, the community does not offer any such program. Strongly moved by the intensity of feeling demonstrated, Town Council members decided to consider the parents' proposal. However, they agreed that rational decision-making requires that program benefits be measured based on the monetary value of recreational services for which households are willing to pay or travel. The Council asked the city manager, as a part of her normal duties, to prepare a cost benefit analysis (CBA) with a 10-year time horizon including discount and participation rate sensitivity.

The assumption is that the proposed program operate on newly purchased land adjoining an existing city park. Generally, the value of volunteer time is entered as a cost. However, in this particular case, organized groups of parents indicate that they would accept full responsibility for the recruitment, training, and scheduling of volunteers. Therefore, the value of volunteer services is used merely to represent shadow prices for benefits received. The value of a specific recreational activity is adjusted upward by the value added in order to adapt an activity for disabled participants.

In social service programs, participation is critical in determining net benefits; therefore, in addition to discount rate sensitivity, this CBA report includes a section on the sensitivity of benefits to different levels of participation.

The proposal calls for the city to build and sponsor a playground and a recreational program for disabled city residents on property adjacent to an existing park. The existing park offers adequate road access and disabled-equipped restrooms. Program costs would include a full-time professional city employee, a half-time groundskeeper, plus cubical and storage area in the existing parks and recreational complex. Property taxes on additional land for the program purchased by the city are forfeited.

Estimated participation numbers represent individuals engaged in a particular team sport, overnight camping, or cross-country skiing, and so forth each year. For example, 50 participants camping out twice in a given year equal 100 participants. We view a 3-day camping activity to consist of 30 participant hours, each hour valued at $10 per participant.

The recreation department is not expected to provide food service and is not responsible for the recruitment or training of volunteers; the decision not to include volunteer hours as a cost implies that these particular volunteers have not diverted their services from elsewhere in the community. However, these volunteers are essential in supplying assistance with team sports, camping, and cross country-skiing (but not for ordinary playground activities) at a rate of one volunteer hour (not a guardian, parent, or companion) per 10 hours of disabled participation. This equals a total of 1,560 volunteer hours (15,600 hours of disabled participants in these 3 activities). The value of each volunteer hour is assumed to be equal to the prevailing minimum wage of $5.50. For example, for six winter seasons, disabled participants engage in a total of 600 hours of cross-country skiing during the 10-year time horizon. This requires 60 volunteer hours or 10 hours per year for a total volunteer benefit of $55 per year when cross-country skiing is available.

Disabled programs often sponsor fundraising recreational events, and, thus, total income derived through such events may be added to the benefit figure. However, expected benefits in the form of grants and donations are not entered in the CBA, presented in Table 11.1; donations or funds raised will be used to offset scholarships for low income participants.

Participants generally will be charged user fees for each recreational program, but not park entrance. These fees are not expected to cover full costs which will be subsidized with tax revenue. For example, even if the user fee was $0.67 per hour for a team sport, the CBA benefit value could be $8. User fees, however, are costs, representing alternative consumption forfeited by participants, their families, or both. The total amount of user fees collected varies with participation, although most program costs are relatively fixed from year to year. Participation estimates are based on potential use by disabled children and adults residing in the municipality.

The Methodology

In the first section of Table 11.1, CBA benefits are based on recreational values derived from sampling. This technique was developed by Ron Watters, by averaging the prices of a national sample of athletic clubs, sport schools, and other commercial recreation service providers. Final dollar values per hour are derived by eliminating the high and low market values and averaging the rest.[1]

Watters' suggestion that volunteer hours represent a benefit needs qualification. In previous chapters, we assumed that volunteer hours allocated to one program represent a cost in terms of alternative community options for their services (volunteers donate their services elsewhere). In this case, the net-value of volunteer hours (dedicated specifically to this program) is used to create a shadow price for the benefit of an enhanced recreation activity for the disabled, not available commercially. The assumption then is that the shadow benefit value of an activity for the disabled is equal to a certain activity's market value plus volunteers needed to make the activity accessible to the disabled.

Realistic estimation of future participation is critical. The actual number of those who potentially might avail themselves of each activity should be considered. The analyst should document a willingness on the part of some advocates to have traveled out-of-town and paid full cost for similar services. Price elasticity of demand is used to estimate usage given a schedule of user fees. The assumption is generally that this project will not adversely affect volunteerism or participation in existing community

Table 11.1 Case study: Cost benefit analysis of a recreational program for the disabled with participation and discount rate sensitivity

# of Years	Activity	Disabled Participation*	Abled Participation*	Total	Hours per Activity	Total Hours	$ per hour Value	Total Yearly Value	Total Value Over Project	Total Disabled Hours
9	Team Sport (S)	300	150	450	40	18000	$8	$144,000	$1,296,000	12000
7	Camping (OC)	100	50	150	30	4500	$10	$45,000	$315,000	3000
6	CC Skiing (CC)	150	75	225	4	900	$6	$5,400	$32,400	600
10	Playground (P)	1500	1125	2625	2	5250	$5	$26,250	$262,500	3000
	All Activities:			3450		28650		$1,905,900		18600

Benefits:

		Year 1	2	3	4	5	6	7	8	9	10	PV (3%)	PV (5%)	PV (7%)
Activities:	Team Sports	$ -	$144,000	$144,000	$144,000	$144,000	$144,000	$144,000	$144,000	$144,000	$144,000			
	Camping	$ -	$ -	$ -	$ 45,000	$ 45,000	$ 45,000	$ 45,000	$ 45,000	$ 45,000	$ 45,000			
	CC Skiing	$ -	$ -	$ 5,400	$ 5,400	$ 5,400	$ 5,400	$ 5,400	$ 5,400	$ -	$ -			
	Playground	$ 13,125	$ 27,708	$ 27,708	$ 27,708	$ 27,708	$ 27,708	$ 27,708	$ 27,708	$ 27,708	$ 27,708			
	Total Activity Benefit	$ 13,125	$171,708	$177,108	$222,108	$222,108	$222,108	$222,108	$222,108	$216,708	$216,708	$1,594,888	$1,424,647	$1,278,247
Volunteers:	Team Sports	$ -	$ 733	$ 733	$ 733	$ 733	$ 733	$ 733	$ 733	$ 733	733			
	Camping	$ -	$ -	$ -	$ 236	$ 236	$ 236	$ 236	$ 236	$ 236	236			
	CC Skiing	$ -	$ -	$ 55	$ 55	$ 55	$ 55	$ 55	55					
	Total Volunteer Benefit	$ -	$ 733	$ 788	$ 1,024	$ 1,024	$ 1,024	$ 1,024	$ 1,024	$ 969	$ 969	7,168	6,396	5,731
Total Benefits:		$ 13,125	$172,442	$177,897	$223,132	$223,132	$223,132	$223,132	$223,132	$217,677	$217,677	$1,602,056	$1,431,042	$1,283,979
Total Benefits (minus 20% drop in participation):		$ 10,500	$137,953	$142,317	$178,506	$178,506	$178,506	$178,506	$178,506	$174,142	$174,142	$1,281,645	$1,144,834	$1,027,183

Costs:												
User Fees:	Team Sports	$ 1,333	$ 1,333	$ 1,333	$ 1,333	$ 1,333	$ 1,333	$ 1,333	$ 1,333	$ 1,333		
	Camping		$ 429	$ 429	$ 429	$ 429	$ 429	$ 429	$ 429	$ 429		
	CC Skiing		$ 100	$ 100	$ 100	$ 100	$ 100	$ 100	$ 100	$ -		
	Total User Fees	$ -	$ 1,333	$ 1,433	$ 1,862	$ 1,862	$ 1,862	$ 1,862	$ 1,862	$ 1,762		
Labor:												
Land:	Purchase	$100,000	$100,000	$100,000	$100,000	$100,000	$100,000	$100,000	$100,000	$100,000		
	Tax Revenue Forfitted	$ 5,000										
Buildings:		$ 400	$ 400	$ 400	$ 400	$ 400	$ 400	$ 400	$ 400	$ 400		
Raw Materials:	Fertilizer	$ 1,500	$ 1,500	$ 1,500	$ 1,500	$ 1,500	$ 1,500	$ 1,500	$ 1,500	$ 1,500		
Equipment:	Athletic and Camping	$ 100	$ 100	$ 100	$ 100	$ 100	$ 100	$ 100	$ 100	$ 100		
Utilities:	Insurance, Driveways,	$ 1,000	$ 1,000	$ 1,000	$ 1,000	$ 1,000	$ 1,000	$ 1,000	$ 1,000	$ 1,000		
	Restrooms, Parking, etc.	$ 34,500	$ 34,500	$ 34,500	$ 34,500	$ 34,500	$ 34,500	$ 34,500	$ 34,500	$ 34,500		
Central Admin:	Feasibility, Supervision,	$ 2,000	$ 1,000	$ 1,000	$ 1,000	$ 1,000	$ 1,000	$ 1,000	$ 1,000	$ 1,000		
	Admin. Assistance											
Tools:		$ 1,000	$ 1,000	$ 1,000	$ 1,000	$ 1,000	$ 1,000	$ 1,000	$ 1,000	$ 1,000		
Media:	Computer, Telephone,	$ 5,000	$ 1,000	$ 1,000	$ 5,000	$ 1,000	$ 1,000	$ 1,000	$ 1,000	$ 1,000		
Residual Value:										$ (4,000)		
Total Costs:		$154,500	$141,833	$141,933	$142,362	$146,362	$142,362	$142,362	$138,262	$1,225,493	$1,110,395	$1,010,950
Total Costs (minus 20% drop in User Fees):		$154,500	$141,567	$141,647	$141,990	$145,990	$141,990	$141,990	$137,910	$1,222,886	$1,108,069	$1,008,866
Net Benefits:										$ 376,563	$ 320,648	$ 273,029
Net Benefit with 20% less participation:										$ 58,759	$ 36,765	$ 18,317

Notes: Sponsors accept participation numbers to include guests. The playground functions for 6 months the first year with pro-rated benefits. Program development and insufficient snowfall limit expected Cross Country Skiing to 6 out of 10 seasons. Volunteers assist with Team Sports, Camping, and CC Skiing at a rate of one volunteer hour (excluding guardian/parent/companion participants) per 10 hours of participation.

Participation numbers represent any individual engaged for one hour in a particular sport, overnight camping, or cross country group event, etc. during the year. For example, fifty participants camping out twice equals 100 participants. Each three-day camping activity equals 30 participant hours valued at $10 per hour per participant.

programs. Base year prices are used throughout the 10-year time horizon; Year 1 = Base Year.

The Analysis

This proposal differentiates "investment," or start-up costs from operating costs. The nature and scope of this proposal are assumed to be separate from programming decisions of the existing recreational department. For CBA consideration, it is necessary to justify project choice, boundaries, the targeted age group, and the potential number of users.

Note that user fees are expected to partially finance these programs. Calculating return on "investment" is not, however, the object of this CBA. The object is to determine if combined private and social benefits exceed both public and private costs. In practice, CBAs of this type will often solve for and present private benefit return based on user fees. Then, in a separate calculation, they determine if the social external benefits to the whole community justify the subsidy.

Conclusion

Net benefits, as presented in Table 11.1, are positive; thus, the proposal deserves serious consideration. However, positive net benefits are heavily dependent both on volunteers and on estimates of participation. CBA methodology does not rely on statistical confidence intervals to deal with such probabilities; net benefits are either positive or negative based on given assumptions. CBA does, as shown in this case study, employ easily interpreted sensitivity analysis for discount rates, participation, and so forth. For example, a simple calculation shows that if resident use in this case study is overestimated by 20%, the total net benefits over a 10-year timeframe averages less than $4,000 per year when discounted at 5%.

APPENDIX

Some Numerical Background

Figure 1.1 in Chapter 1 indicates that cost benefit analysis (CBA) solves for the present value of net benefits [NPV (B)] by subtracting discounted costs [GPV (C)] from discounted benefits [GPV (B)]. This Appendix, with the assistance of Microsoft Office Excel, is designed as a tutorial in discounting costs and benefits to determine the present value of net benefits.

The net present value (NPV) technique assumes that a dollar presently held by a local community is worth more than a dollar's worth of benefits received in the future. Consider any positive rate of interest, say 10%. A year from now that dollar would be worth $1.10 in which case more than $1.00 worth of benefits could be purchased. Also, the dollar held at present will be able to cover $1.10 in future costs. Therefore, any dollars paid or received in the future must first be discounted to determine the net present value of a project's benefits.

Consider the following project given an interest or discount rate of 5%:

Time Period	Expected Benefits	Expected Costs
1	100	300
2	300	100
3	400	100

Open a spreadsheet and enter the following data:

	A	B	C	D	E	F	G
1		Year One	Year Two	Year Three	Discount Rate	Present Value	
2	Expected Costs:	300	100	100	5%		
3							
4							
5							
6	Expected Benefits:	100	300	400	5%		
7							
8							
9							
10					Net PV Benefits		
11							

To calculate the PV of **costs**, in Cell F2, type = and search for the NPV function. Enter the Function Arguments for expected costs and press OK:

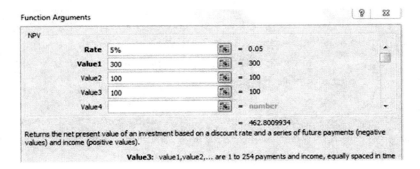

Function Arguments

NPV

Rate	5%		= 0.05
Value1	300		= 300
Value2	100		= 100
Value3	100		= 100
Value4			= number

= 462.8009934

Returns the net present value of an investment based on a discount rate and a series of future payments (negative values) and income (positive values).

Value3: value1,value2,... are 1 to 254 payments and income, equally spaced in time

To calculate the PV of **benefits**, in Cell F6, type = and search for the NPV function. Enter the Function Arguments for expected benefits and press OK:

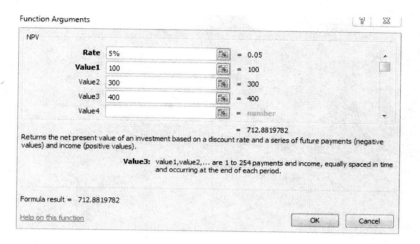

In Cell F10 on your worksheet, you will calculate Net PV Benefits. These are equal to F6 (the present value of expected benefits) minus F2 (the present value of expected costs). Note that net benefits in this example are positive and equal $250.08. Such a proposal exceeds the cost benefit hurdle and is worthy of consideration.

	A	B	C	D	E	F	G
1		Year One	Year Two	Year Three	Discount Rate	Present Value	
2	**Expected Costs:**	300	100	100	5%	$462.80	
3							
4							
5							
6	**Expected Benefits:**	100	300	400	5%	$712.88	
7							
8							
9							
10					**Net PV Benefits**	$250.08	
11							

Theoretically, net benefits (benefits minus costs) could be calculated for each year and then discounted, but standard practice in CBA is to list and discount costs and benefits separately.

Notes

Chapter 1

1. Gramlich (1990), p. 223.
2. Ray (1984), p. 9.
3. Buchanan and Tullock (1999), p. 32.

Chapter 2

1. Dasgupta and Pearce (1972).
2. Sugden (2007).
3. Mishan and Quah (2007).
4. Scotchmer (2002).
5. Boudreaux (2013).
6. Adler (2012).
7. Harberger (2010a).

Chapter 4

1. Flyvbjerg, Holm, and Buhl (2002).
2. Boardman, Greenberg, Vining, and Weimer (1997), p. 370.
3. McIntosh, Clarke, Frew, and Louviere (2010), p. 107

Chapter 5

1. Harberger, *Addressing social concerns* (2008b) online.
2. Pearce, D.W. *Cost-Benefit Analysis* (1983), p. 3
3. Harberger, *Addressing social concerns* (2008b) online.
4. Little and Mirrlees (1994).

Chapter 6

1. Scotchmer (2002).
2. Harberger (2010b), p. 8–9.
3. Vining and Weimer (2010).

Chapter 7

1. Whitesides (2011).
2. Vining and Weimer (2010).
3. Ewert (2000).
4. Lambur, Rajgopal, Lewis, Cox, and Ellerbrock (2003).
5. Elliot, Holt, and Moore (2002).

Chapter 8

1. Gramlich (1990), p. 198
2. Moore (1998), p. 50.
3. Moore (1998), p. 53.
4. Moore (1998), p. 55.
5. Cowen (1998).

Chapter 9

1. South Bend Tribune (2011).

Chapter 10

1. Probst (2009).

Chapter 11

1. Watters (1991).

Bibliography

Adler, M. D. (2012). *Well-being and fair distribution: Beyond cost-benefit analysis.* New York, NY: Oxford University Press.

Adler, M. D., & Posner, E. A. (1999). *Rethinking cost-benefit analysis* John M. Olin Law & Economics Working Paper #72, University of Chicago Law School.

Arrow, K. J., & Lind, R. C. (2003). Risk and uncertainty: Uncertainty and the evaluation of public investment decisions. In R. Layard & S. Glaister (Eds.), *Cost-benefit analysis* (IInd ed.) (pp. 160–178). New York, NY: Cambridge University Press.

Boudreaux, D. J. (2013, April 24). Thank you for smoking. *The Wall Street Journal.*

Breidert, C., Hahsler, M., & Reutterer, T. (2006). A review of methods for measuring willingness to pay. *Innovation Marketing 2* (4), 8–32.

Boardman, A. E., Greenberg, D. H., Vining, A. R., & Weimer, D. L. (1997). Plus-in' shadow price estimates for policy analysis. *Annals of Regional Science 31*, 299–324.

Buchanan, J. M., & Tullock, G. (1999). *The calculus of consent: Logical foundations of constitutional democracy.* Indianapolis, IN: Liberty Fund.

Commonwealth of Australia (2006). *Handbook of Cost-Benefit Analysis.* Public Law Financial Management Reference Material No. 6, 164.

Cowen, T. (1998). *Using cost-benefit analysis to review regulation.* Draft Chapter prepared at George Mason University. https://www.gmu.edu/centers/publicchoice/faculty%20pages/Tyler/Cowen%20on%20cost%20benefit.pdf

Dasgupta, A. K., & Pearce, D. W. (1972). *Cost-benefit analysis: Theory and practice* (Macmillan student editions). London and Basingstoke: The Macmillan Press Ltd.

De Alessi, L. (1996). Error and bias in benefit-cost analysis: HUD's case for the wind rule. *Cato Journal 16*(1), 129–147.

Elliot, D., Holt, G. E., & Moore, A. (2002). *Results of the cost/benefit analysis survey of skokie public library in 2002.* Institute of Museum and Library Services.

Elliott, D.S. 2007. *Measuring Your Library's Value.* Chicago: American Library Association.

Engineering Solutions On-Line. (2013). *Cost benefit analysis template.* Retrieved from http://download.cnet.com/Cost-Benefit-Analysis-Template

European Commission Directorate General Regional Policy. (2008). *Guide to cost benefit analysis of investment projects*. Retrieved February 22, 2012, from http:// ec.europa.eu/regional_policy/sources/docgener/guides/cost/ guide2008_en.pdf

Ewert, A. (2000). Outdoor recreation at 40: An essential ingredient in the outdoor recreation mix. *Parks and Recreation 37*(8), 64–72.

Ferlic, F. (2011, August 8). Testing consolidation of animal control makes sense. *South Bend Tribune*.

Flyvbjerg, B., Holm, M. S., & Buhl, S. (2002). Underestimating costs in public works projects: Error or lies. *Journal of the American Planning Association 68*(3), 279–295.

Gramlich, E. M. (1990). *A guide to benefit-cost analysis* (IInd ed). Englewood Cliffs, NJ: Prentice Hall.

Harberger, A. C. (2008a). *Introduction to cost-benefit analysis part II: Labor market issues*. Retrieved October 23, 2011, from University of California: http:// www.econ.ucla.edu/harberger/

Harberger, A. C. (2008b). *Introduction to cost-benefit analysis part III: Addressing social concerns*. Retrieved October 23, 2011, from University of California: http://www.econ.ucla.edu/harberger/

Harberger, A. C. (2008c). *Introduction to cost-benefit analysis part IV: Applications to highway projects*. Retrieved October 23, 2011, from University of California: http://www.econ.ucla.edu/harberger/

Harberger, A. C. (2009). *Introduction to cost-benefit analysis part V: Applications to irrigation projects*. Retrieved October 23, 2011, from University of California: http://www.econ.ucla.edu/harberger/

Harberger, A. C. (2010a). *Applied welfare economics in practice*. Retrieved October 23, 2011, from University of California: http://www.econ.ucla.edu/ harberger/

Harberger, A. C. (2010b). *More on the cost-benefit analysis of electricity projects*. Retrieved October 23, 2011, from University of California: http://www. econ.ucla.edu/harberger/

HM Treasury. (2003). *Green book*. London, UK: TSO.

Keating, B. P., & Keating, M. O. (2009). *Microeconomics for public managers*. Oxford, UK: Wiley-Blackwell.

Kendall, M. G. (1971). *Cost-benefit analysis*. A symposium held in the Hague in July, 1969 under the aegis of the NATO Scientific Affairs Committee. New York, NY: American Elsevier Publishing Company, Inc.

Lambur, M., Rajgopal, R., Lewis. E., Cox, R. H., & Ellerbrock, M. (2003). *Applying cost benefit analysis to nutrition programs: Focus on the virginia expanded food and nutrition education program* (Report Number 490–403). Virginia Cooperative Extension.

Layard, R., & Glaister, S. (1994). *Cost-benefit analysis* (IInd ed.) (pp. 1–56). New York, NY: Cambridge University Press.

Litman, T. A., & Doherty, E. (2009). *Transportation cost and benefit analysis: Techniques, estimates and implications* (IInd ed.). Victoria, CA: Victoria Transport Policy Institute.

Little, I. M. D., & Mirrlees, J. A. (1994). The costs and benefits of analysis: Project appraisal and planning twenty years. In R. Layard & S. Glaister (Eds.), *Cost-benefit analysis* (pp. 199–231). New York, NY: Cambridge University Press.

McIntosh, E., Clarke, P. M., Frew, E. J., & Louviere, J. J. (2010). *Applied methods of cost-benefit analysis in health care.* Oxford, UK: Oxford University Press.

McKenzie, R. B., & Lee, D. R. (2010). *Microeconomics for MBAs: The economic way of thinking for managers* (IInd ed.). Cambridge, UK: Cambridge University Press.

Mishan, E. J. (1976). *Elements of cost-benefit analysis* (IInd ed.). London, UK: George Allen and Unwin Ltd.

Mishan, E. J., & Quah, E. (2007). *Cost-benefit analysis* (Vth ed.). Oxford, UK: Routledge, Taylor & Francis e-library.

Moore, A. T. (1998). Indianapolis's road to regulatory reform: A new path in licensing and permits. *Regulation (Winter)*, 49–56.

Pearce, D. W. (1983). *Cost-benefit analysis* (IInd ed.). New York, NY: St. Martin's Press.

Probst, A. (2009). *Cost/benefit analysis.* Financial Analyst Series, Vol. Series Number 14, Local Government Center, UW-Extension.

Ray, A. (1984). *Cost-benefit analysis: Issues and methodologies.* Baltimore, MD: The Johns Hopkins University Press.

Robinson, L., & Hammitt, J. K. (2011). Behavioral economics and the conduct of benefit-cost analysis: Towards principles and standards. *Journal of Benefit-Cost Analysis 2*(2), 1–48.

Schmidtz, D. (2001). A place for cost-benefit analysis. *Philosophical Issues 11*(1), 148–171.

Scotchmer, S. (2002). Local public goods and clubs. In A. J. Auerbach & M. Feldstein (Eds.), *Handbook of public economics.* Amsterdam, NL: EsevierScience B.V.

Sugden, R. (2007). *Cost-benefit analysis as market simulation: A new approach to the problem of anomalies in environmental evaluation (A previous version of paper was present at the conference 'Frontiers of Environmental Economics' organized by Resources for the Future in Washington, D.C., 26–27 February 2007)* Retrieved September 6, 2011, from http://papers.ssrn.com/sol3/papers.cfm?abstract_id=1004778

U.S. Office of Management and Budget. (1992). *Circular A-94: Guidelines and discount rates for benefit-cost analysis of federal programs.* Retrieved October 26, 2011, from www.whitehouse.gov/omb/circulars_a094

U.S. Office of Management and Budget. (2003). *Circular A-4: Regulatory analysis.* Retrieved October 26, 2011, from http://www.whitehouse.gov/sites/default/files/omb/assets/regulatory_matters_pdf/a-4.pdf

United Nations. (1972). *Guidelines for project evaluation.* (Project formulation and evaluation series, no. 2). New York, NY: United Nations.

Vining, A., & David, L. W. (2010). An assessment of important issues concerning the application of benefit-cost analysis to social policy. *Journal of Benefit-Cost Analysis 1*(1), 1–38.

Watkins, T. (2011). *An introduction to cost benefit analysis.* Retrieved December 8, 2011, from http://www.sjsu.edu/faculty/watkins/cba.htm

Watters, R. (1991). *Cost benefit analysis of recreation program for the disabled.* Pocatello, ID: Idaho State University Outdoor Program.

Whitesides, G. (2011, November 17). The frugal way: The promise of cost-conscious science. *The Economist,* p. 154.

Wolfe, J. N. (1973). *Cost benefit and cost effectiveness: Studies and analysis.* London: George Allen & Unwin LTD.

Index

OTHER TITLES FROM THE ECONOMICS COLLECTION

Philip Romero, The University of Oregon and
Jeffrey Edwards, North Carolina A&T State University, Editors

- *Regression for Economics, Second Edition* by Shahdad Naghshpour
- *Eastern European Economies: A Region in Transition* by Marcus Goncalves and Erika Cornelius Smith
- *Health Financing Without Deficits: Reform That Sidesteps Political Gridlock* by Philip J. Romero and Randy S. Miller
- *Central and Eastern European Economies: Perspectives and Challenges* by Marcus Goncalves And Erika Cornelius Smith
- *A Primer on Non-Parametric Analysis, Volume I* by Shahdad Naghshpour
- *A Primer on Non-Parametric Analysis, Volume II* by Shahdad Naghshpour
- *The Modern Caribbean Economy: Alternative Perspectives and Policy Implications, Volume I* by Nikolaos Karagiannis and Debbie A. Mohammed
- *The Modern Caribbean Economy: Economic Development and Public Policy Challenges, Volume II* by Nikolaos Karagiannis And Debbie A. Mohammed
- *How the Information Revolution Remade Business and the Economy: A Roadmap for Progress of the Semiconductor Industry* by Apek Mulay
- *Money and Banking: An Intermediate Market-Based Approach, Second Edition* by William D. Gerdes

Announcing the Business Expert Press Digital Library

Concise e-books business students need for classroom and research

This book can also be purchased in an e-book collection by your library as

- a one-time purchase,
- that is owned forever,
- allows for simultaneous readers,
- has no restrictions on printing, and
- can be downloaded as PDFs from within the library community.

Our digital library collections are a great solution to beat the rising cost of textbooks. E-books can be loaded into their course management systems or onto students' e-book readers.
The **Business Expert Press** digital libraries are very affordable, with no obligation to buy in future years. For more information, please visit **www.businessexpertpress.com/librarians**. To set up a trial in the United States, please email **sales@businessexpertpress.com**.

CPSIA information can be obtained
at www.ICGtesting.com
Printed in the USA
FSOW02n0700200617
35402FS